The
Woman's Day
Book of Salads

Carol Truax's previous books:

Five Hundred Super Stews
Gourmet Entertaining on a Budget
The Woman's Day Book of Thin Italian Cooking
The Art of Salad Making
The Weekend Chef
The Cattleman's Steak Book
The Sixty Minute Chef
Liberace Cooks
Father Was a Gourmet
The Woman's Day Chicken Cookbook
Cooking with Wine and Cheese
Soups and Sandwiches
Desserts
Gourmet Cooking on a Budget

EDITOR:
The Ladies Home Journal Cookbook
The Ladies Home Journal Dessert Cookbook

THE
Woman's Day
BOOK OF
Salads

Carol Truax

E. P. DUTTON / New York

For information contact: E. P. Dutton, 2 Park Avenue, New York, N.Y. 10016.

Recipes tested and edited by Bonnie Levine.

Published simultaneously in Canada by Clarke, Irwin & Company Limited, Toronto and Vancouver
10 9 8 7 6 5 4 3 2 1
First Edition

Library of Congress Cataloging in Publication Data
Truax, Carol.
    The Woman's day book of salads.
    1. Salads. I. Woman's day. II. Title.
TX740.T78   641.8′3   79-27146

ISBN: 0-525-93127-9

Contents

Preface

Everyone wants to eat well, look great, and be healthy; we are all interested in good food and good nutrition. With salads we need not sacrifice either flavor or nutrients. Gone are the days when a gourmet was almost certain to be a gourmand, and obesity was often the result of elegant dining.

At the beginning of this century, dinner at a fashionable club might have involved nine courses, including caviar, goose liver, soup, salmon, stuffed partridge, roast lamb, cheese, and a rich dessert. Even cooks who prided themselves on their good, simple meals expected to spend many hours of each day in the kitchen.

Today's homemaker cares as much, if not more, about what is put on her table than her mother did twenty years ago. But food is now in keeping with a more modern life-style, streamlined eating that combines good nutrition and easy preparation with a concern for weight control. To reach this goal, salads are the perfect food. Salads are so versatile that they can be eaten *with* the meal, substituting for any course on the menu, or *as* the meal itself. There are salads for each part of any meal, from appetizer to dessert. Salads can be hearty or light, zesty or bland, rich or refreshing, simple or elaborate, and salads can inconspicuously adapt themselves to almost any dietary problem or whim without making the cook feel she needs the help of a trained nutritionist to create a

1

healthy, satisfying meal. Meat, poultry, fish, cheese, nuts, eggs, and beans are all sources of protein and can all be included in the preparation of a tasty salad.

Fresh produce can now travel cross-country in as little time as it would take to come from a local farm. Progress has also been made in commercial canning and freezing, and "putting up" fruits and vegetables at home is no longer the tedious process it used to be. Home freezing methods are simple enough so that the modern cook can take advantage of the season when flavors are highest and the prices are lowest. And there are many newly popular ingredients, such as sprouts and yogurt, to stimulate the salad-maker's imagination.

Salads decorate the table and add sparkle and zest to any menu; they stimulate, supplement, and *satisfy*.

NOTE: When a recipe is marked with an asterisk (*) it can be found in the index. Green onions are frequently scallions. See Onions, page 22.

How to Select and Care for Fruits and Vegetables

The selection, storage, and care of fruits and vegetables, the main ingredients in salad-making, are very important for the salad-chef. Salads are not usually cooked, and the natural flavors of the foods are very evident. Only the very best produce should ever be used in a salad.

The most commonly used fruits and vegetables are:

Anise	Chayotes	Jerusalem artichokes
Apples	Cherries	
Apricots	Chinese cabbage	Kiwi
Artichokes	Chives	Kohlrabi
Asparagus	Coconuts	Kumquats
Avocados	Corn, sweet	
	Cranberries	Leeks
Bananas	Crenshaws	Lemons
Beans, green	Cucumbers	Lettuce
Beans, lima		Limes
Beets	Dasheens	Litchis
Berries	Dates	
Blueberries		Mangoes
Broccoli	Eggplants	Melons
Brussels sprouts	Endive-Escarole-Chicory	Mushrooms
	Figs	
Cabbage		Nectarines
Cantaloupes	Grapefruit	
Carrots	Grapes	Okra
Casabas	Greens	Onions, dry
Cauliflower	Guavas	Onions, green
Celeriac		Oranges
Celery	Honeydews	
	Horseradish root	Papayas

3

Parsley
Parsnips
Peaches
Pears
Peas, green
Peppers, sweet
Persians
Persimmons
Pineapples
Plantains
Plums and Italian prunes

Pomegranates
Potatoes
Pumpkins

Radishes
Rhubarb
Rutabagas

Shallots
Spinach
Squash

Strawberries
Sweet potatoes

Tangelos
Tangerines
Tomatoes
Turnips

Uglifruit

Watermelons
Watercress

To select fresh fruits and vegetables of good quality some information about each food is desirable. A few general principles of selection and care that may be helpful follow:

FRESHNESS: Buy only fruits and vegetables that *look fresh* and reasonably unblemished. Wilted, wrinkled, drooping, insect-damaged, or dirty produce should be rejected.

COLOR: *Look for items of characteristic color.* Often color is a good guide to quality, and information about it is included below.

SHAPE: Shape is also important. Grossly misshapen fruits and vegetables usually are inferior in texture and taste and certainly are wasteful. They are more difficult to prepare.

SIZE: In general, the medium sizes are preferred for most purposes. Items extremely large or extremely small may have undesirable points. For example, very large fruits may be coarse and overmature. On the other hanu, extremely small ones may be immature and will have too much waste in relation to the edible portion.

MATURITY: The maturity of a fruit or vegetable can be defined as the state at which it is judged right for harvesting in order to bring it to the consumer in best possible condition. Such maturity varies. All leafy vegetables must be immature. If they carry seed-bearing parts, they are too mature and will be tough. In the case of "fruit" (using this term in the botanical sense to include all seed-containing plant parts such as peaches, apples, tomatoes, cucumbers, peppers, squash), degree of maturity is an important factor in selection. Most states have laws regulating maturity at which harvesting is to occur.

Ripeness is different from maturity. For many products, "ripeness" is undesirable: for example, a ripe cucumber would have hard seeds, poor flavor, and be inedible. For others, such as peaches, moderate ripeness is desirable.

TOPS: Root vegetables should be bought without the tops unless the tops are to be eaten. There is no reason to buy them if they are to be thrown away. On the other hand, tops that are young, tender, and green are tasty and highly nutritious. The tops of some vegetables can be toxic.

GRADES: Grades of fresh fruits and vegetables apply to commercial operations. They are useful to shippers, wholesalers, and large-scale buyers, but the consumer must rely on the senses—mainly sight—to select from what is offered.

JUDGMENT: Avoid being taken in by such statements as "organically grown" fruits and vegetables. Often they are priced at 50 percent to 100 percent more than other fruits and vegetables and they are in no way superior—and sometimes are inferior. Rely on your own good judgment of appearance and price; ignore fancy claims made without the slightest factual support. (More about this later.)

STORAGE: Fresh fruits and vegetables should be bought for use within a short time. Some fruits must be held to soften and ripen. Long storage at home, however, is not practical. Extended storage requires special equipment and detailed knowledge.

TEMPERATURE: This book deals only with what can be done by anyone who has an ordinary kitchen and a standard modern refrigerator or even one not so modern. In many cases, I suggest keeping a vegetable "cold and humid." This means a temperature as near to 32° F as possible and high humidity, but not wet. Most home refrigerators provide temperatures in the general compartment of around 40° F and the temperature can be regulated up or down.

HUMIDITY: High humidity can be achieved by keeping the commodity in a plastic bag or in a hydrator compartment, or both. Many fruits and vegetables are bought in plastic and may be kept in them. In some cases I suggest keeping a commodity "cool," which means in the neighborhood of 50° F to 60° F. It is realized that in most cases the homeowner can only choose either to refrigerate or not to refrigerate. In an air-conditioned room, however, there will be places out of the sun and away from other sources of heat that can be called "cool." In some cases I suggest keeping a commodity "dry." This does not mean desert aridity but rather exposing it to the air of the ordinary room or open to the movement of air in the refrigerator so that surface moisture will evaporate. Do not keep produce wet or so moist as to show droplets of water.

PREPACKAGING: A prepacked unit using the right type of film for the particular item is desirable to protect produce, but a package is not a substitute for either initial high quality of the contents or refrigeration. Proper temperature from shipping point to consumer is essential and is the most important single element in marketing fresh produce.

PRICE: Prices of fresh produce vary widely depending on supply, and in most cases supply depends largely on the season. Fresh fruits and vegetables are generally not only lowest in price but highest in quality when they are most abundant.

The following list of fruits and vegetables includes general advice on the care and storage of the produce. But, if there are directions on the wrapper, follow those directions as closely as possible.

ANISE: This salad and cooking vegetable has a bulb and a feathery top. The foliage should be fresh and green and the stalk and bulb firm and of a light greenish-white color. Anise has an aniselike flavor, hence the name. Keep cold and humid and use within a few days. Available October through April.

APPLES: For the fruit bowl and raw in salads: Delicious, Golden Delicious, Cortland, McIntosh, Newtown, Northern Spy, Stayman, Winesap, Jonathan, Gravenstein, Grimes Golden (which are very scarce). For pie, sauce, and other cooking: McIntosh, Newtown, Northern Spy, Rhode Island Greening, Wealthy, Stayman, York, Golden Delicious. For baking: Rome Beauty, McIntosh, Rhode Island Greening, Stayman, York, Jonathan, and Wealthy are tasty and attractive looking.

There is no agreement on which apple varieties should be used for what. Actually, any apple can be used for any purpose, but results will vary.

For apples to be eaten out of the hand or in salads, mature fruit is desirable. For cooking, many prefer green or at least not quite ripe apples, but note that Newtown is greenish yellow when mature and Rhode Island Greening is brighter green.

Apples should be firm, unbruised, not wilted or punctured, and of good color. If the "bite test" shows apples for eating raw need ripening, leave them at room temperature for a day or two or more, then refrigerate. Apples from cold storage often have flavor comparable to those from tree to consumer. Apples like cold and high humidity. Keep and use as desired. Available all year.

APRICOTS: This is a delicate fruit and cannot be shipped when fully ripe. Favor fruits that are plump and relatively soft though not damaged. Select fruit that is orange yellow and pass up greenish apricots. Keep cold and humid and use within two or three days. Available mostly in June and July.

ARTICHOKES: Choose compact, heavy, plump globes that have large, tightly clinging, fleshy leaf scales of a green color. Keep cold and humid and use within a few days. Available all year with the peak season in April through May. (This is no relation of the Jerusalem artichoke, which is discussed later.)

ASPARAGUS: The green portion of fresh asparagus is the most tender, so select stalks with largest amount of green. Stalks should be fresh, firm, with compact closed tips. Open tips are a sign of overmaturity. Angular or flat stalks are apt to be woody.

This vegetable should be kept cold all the way to the consumer. Warm asparagus should be viewed with suspicion as they are likely to be turning fibrous. Reject asparagus that have their butt soaking in water or appear to have been soaked. At home keep asparagus cold and humid and use as soon as possible. Available March into June.

Avocados: Avocados on the market are mature but that does not mean ripe. They are picked according to percentage of oil content. Firm or hard avocados are all right to buy but they must be kept at room temperature until soft, before they are eaten. The fruit should be bright and fresh-looking, heavy for its size, not wilted or bruised. Irregular brown marks are superficial and do not affect quality. Color ranges from purple black to green, according to variety. After the fruit is soft-ripe, refrigerate until used. Available all year.

Bananas: Good quality bananas at retail may be anything from partly green to all yellow with brown spots. Fruit should be plump, not bruised or split. If not ripe, ripen at room temperature. Bananas ripen ideally off the plant and even for consumption where grown are harvested green. Pay no attention to advice that bananas must have brown spots before being eaten.

To ripen, leave them in a bowl or dish and wait until they reach the stage you prefer. If they are sold in a plastic bag, open the bag. When ripened, bananas can be refrigerated. The skin will turn brown in time from refrigeration but the flesh keeps well for two or more days after ripening. Available all year.

Beans, green: Should be fresh and green in appearance, free from scars and discoloration, and break with a snap. They should have no strings, and the seeds should be immature. Keep beans cold and humid and use as soon as possible. (Same for wax beans.) Available all year with peak May through August.

Beans, lima: Supplies are small. If in the pod, the pods should be fresh, well filled, bright, and dark green. Shelled limas should be plump with tender skin of a green or greenish-white color. Keep cold and humid and use as soon as possible. Limas are highly perishable. Available mostly May into October.

BEETS: Early beets are often marketed in bunches with the tops on. If tops are fresh and unblemished, they make good eating. Late crop beets are usually sold topped. Select small or medium-size roots that are firm and of good color. Large beets may be woody. Flabby, rough, or shriveled beets are undesirable. Remove and use greens as soon as possible; use the roots within a week. Keep cold and humid. Available all year with peak June through October.

BERRIES (MISCELLANEOUS): Blackberries, raspberries, strawberries, boysenberries, loganberries, and others need to be fresh, cold, dry, and free of bruising and mold, and should not show signs of leaking. Keep cold and covered and use as soon as possible. Available mostly June through August.

BROCCOLI: It should be fresh and green with compact bud clusters that have not opened to show the yellow flowers. The color can be dark green, sage green, or purple green. Stalks and stems should appear green and fresh. Yellowed and wilted leaves indicate old age. Keep cold and humid and use as soon as possible. Available all year with period of greatest abundancy October through May.

BRUSSELS SPROUTS: Good sprouts are firm, compact, fresh bright green. Puffy or soft sprouts are poor eating. Wilted or yellow leaves indicate aging. Keep cold and humid and use as soon as possible. Peak period of availability is September through February.

CABBAGE: Heads should be reasonably solid and heavy in relation to size, and closely trimmed, with stems cut close to the head, only three or four outer or wrapper leaves, and no loose leaves. Do not expect early cabbage to be as solid as a late crop. *Outer leaves should be green.* Green cabbage is more nutritious than white. Cabbage with worm injury, yellowing leaves, splits, or softness and puffiness should be rejected. Heads with some outer leaves separated from the stem may have undesirably strong flavor and be coarse textured.

Red cabbage is selected the same way as the green except for color; and savoy cabbage with naturally wrinkled leaves selected the same way except for leaf texture. Long, pointed cabbage differs mainly in shape, but the leaves are also smoother than other types.

All cabbage should be kept cold and humid and used within a week or two. Cabbage is on the market all year in large amounts.

CANTALOUPES: If a cantaloupe has been picked at the right time, it will ripen well, and it will have a smoothly rounded, depressed scar at the stem end. This is called the "full slip" condition, because the stem has come off fully and smoothly. If the stem end is rough with portions of the stem adhering, the cantaloupe probably was not fully mature when picked. If the melons have been shipped a long way, as most are, they must be picked while firm; at full slip they have developed their full sugar content and need only to soften. This process may take three or four days *at room temperature.*

Give them time to take on a yellow appearance and acquire a distinctive aroma. A really well-ripened cantaloupe is worth waiting for. When ripe, refrigerate if they are not to be eaten immediately. Some people like cantaloupes served at room temperature. Available mainly June through September.

CARROTS: The readily available packs of topped carrots in

plastic bags are usually satisfactory. The carrots should be firm, fresh, smooth, well shaped, and of a good orange color. Wilted, flabby, soft, or shriveled carrots are undesirable. Bunches of fresh small carrots are especially desirable. Keep cold and humid and use as desired. On the market all year in large amounts.

CASABAS: The casaba is a large, heavy, almost globular melon, light green to yellow but definitely yellow when ripe. It has a tough rind profusely marked with longitudinal deep wrinkles. In addition to color, ripeness is indicated by slight softening at the stem end. In a ripe melon of good quality the flesh is soft, creamy white, sweet, and juicy. Keep cool and avoid drying out. Available July through November in small quantities with peak in September and October.

CAULIFLOWER: Good quality is indicated by a white or creamy-white clean, firm, compact curd. Most cauliflower is shipped with no jacket leaves, but if there are any leaves, they should be fresh and green. Size of the head has no relation to quality. Avoid loose, open flower clusters because they indicate overmaturity. Also avoid spotted or speckled heads or those with brown areas, which indicate bruising. A slightly "ricey" granular appearance does not affect quality provided the flower clusters are compact. Keep cold and humid and use as soon as possible. On the market all year in fairly large amounts.

CELERIAC: This is often referred to as celery root or celery knob and is a variety of celery. It should be firm and free from damage. Keep it cold and humid. On the market all year but mostly October through April.

CELERY: Most celery on the market is of the Pascal type and has green outer stalks. Celery should be fresh, crisp, clean, with stalks that are thick and solid. Soft, somewhat pliable branches often indicate pithiness and indicate lack of freshness. On the other hand, excessively hard branches may be stringy or woody. Celery with seed stems is undesirably mature. Such seed stems may appear as a solid somewhat round stem replacing the heart formation. Avoid celery with discoloration of the small, center branches. Keep cold and humid and use as desired. On the market all year in large amounts.

CHAYOTES: A relative of the cucumber, chayotes produce pear-shaped fruit three to five inches long, ranging from dark green to ivory white. It is sometimes called the vegetable pear. The fruit should be fresh-looking, not deeply wrinkled. Keep them cool and humid. On the market in very small amounts mostly November through May.

CHERRIES: Look for fruit that is fresh, firm, highly colored ranging from bright red to black, not sticky. Cherries with any decay should be rejected. Immature fruit is hard, lighter in color than the ripe, usually smaller, and is acidic and dry. It will not ripen. Keep cold and humid and use in two or three days. On the market late May into August.

CHINESE CABBAGE: Heads are conical and should be compact with crisp, clean, fresh, green, not yellowing or wilted leaves. Keep cold and humid and use within a week or so. On the market all year.

CHIVES: This relative of onions, but milder in flavor, is often sold growing in pots. The pots will supply fresh chive leaves for several weeks if given good care. Chives are also available in bunches. The "season" is whenever you can find them, usually in the spring.

COCONUTS: Look for nuts that are heavy for their size and full of liquid. Shake the nut and make sure the nutritious juice sloshes around. If the nut is dry, reject it. Nuts with moldy or wet "eyes" are not good. Keep nuts cold and use as soon as possible. They are on the market all year, but more readily available September through December.

CORN, SWEET: Most corn now on the market is yellow. It has considerable vitamin A, while white corn has less. Try to obtain true "sweet" corn, not immature field corn.

Sweet corn, to be good, must be kept cold from immediately after it is harvested to the kitchen kettle. Corn that is warm to the touch should be rejected. It will almost certainly taste starchy, and the kernels may be tough. The sugar in corn turns to starch with time and warmth, and it doesn't take long. If the corn has husks, the husks should be fresh and green, not dry and straw-colored. Keep cold and humid until used, and use as soon as possible. The very abundant corn in summer, from close by, is the most satisfactory. It is on the market all year, but more in the late summer and early fall.

CRANBERRIES: These berries generally are of good quality when they reach the market, so buying is not a problem. Packing houses have a method of rejecting berries of poor color and texture. Look for fresh, plump, lustrous, firm berries, red to reddish black. Refrigerate and use within a week or two, or freeze in the original package and use any time. Available September through December.

CRENSHAWS: This is a hybrid muskmelon weighing seven to nine pounds. It is round at the base and comes to a point at the stem end. It has a gold and green rind that is smooth with no netting and little ribbing. The meat is a bright salmon color, thick, juicy, and very good when ripe. A ready-to-eat melon shows softening of the rind, especially at the large end, and has a golden skin and rich aroma. Keep at room temperature until ripe, then keep cool and use soon. Available July to October with peak in August and September.

CUCUMBERS: Avoid cukes that have a yellow color, which indicates old age. Also avoid very large cucumbers, which also are likely to have hard seeds. They should have soft and immature seeds. Reject withered or shriveled cucumbers or ones that show any puffiness. Keep cool and humid and use within a few days. Available all year with peak May through August.

DASHEENS: The dasheen is a tropical plant with edible corms and tubers that is grown to a small extent in the South. It was formerly called Oriental taro. First-grade tubers are ovoid and smooth and weigh from four to eight ounces each. The corms are somewhat spherical, the tubers ovoid-cylindrical. Tubers keep better than corms. Both need to be cool and dry. In New York City they are on the market all year.

DATES: Fruit should be lustrous-brown and soft. They are prepackaged and available either pitted or with pits. When package is opened, refrigerate. Keep them well wrapped to avoid drying and hardening, and use as desired. On the market all year.

EGGPLANTS: They should be firm, heavy for their size, with a dark purple to purple-black skin. (There are light-colored eggplants on the market.) They should be free of scars or cuts. A wilted, shriveled, soft, or flabby fruit will not only be wasteful, but usually is bitter or otherwise poor in flavor. Fruit with worm injury on the surface should be rejected. Keep cool and humid and use as soon as possible. On the market all year with peak in August and September.

ENDIVE-ESCAROLE-CHICORY: Like all greens, they should be fresh, clean, crisp, and cold. They should not have dry or yellowing leaves or seed stems, which mean old age. Flabby and wilted leaves also can mean old age or poor care. The bunches should not show black or otherwise discolored leaf margins or reddish discoloration of the hearts. Keep cold and humid and use as soon as possible. On the market all year.

FIGS: Fresh figs, available in very small amounts in some stores, mainly August to October, should be soft-ripe and have characteristic color that ranges from greenish yellow to purple or black, depending on variety. Overripeness is indicated by softness and a sour odor. Keep cold and use immediately. They are extremely perishable.

GRAPEFRUIT: The trend is toward seedless grapefruit. It makes sense to choose seedless, since the edible portion is much larger than in the seedy fruit. As to whether white or pink should be chosen, that is a matter of taste. The white is usually stronger in flavor than the pink. Good grapefruits are firm, springy to the touch, not soft, wilted, flabby, puffy, or loose-skinned. They should be globular and heavy for their size. Heavy fruits are thin-skinned and contain more juice than the thick-skinned. Fruits somewhat pointed at the stem end tend to be thick-skinned. Russeting does no harm nor does it matter whether the skin is bronze colored. Medium to large fruits are preferred for segmenting. Grapefruits are ready to eat, since only mature fruit is shipped. They may be kept at room temperature or refrigerated and used as desired. On the market all year.

GRAPES: All grapes are as ripe when bought as they will be so don't buy any with the thought of holding them to "ripen." Only ready-to-eat grapes are shipped. Grapes should be firmly attached to the stem. If the stem is dry and brittle, the grapes tend to fall off. The fruit should appear fresh, smooth, plump, not sticky; and the grapes should be well colored for the variety, that is, amber-green Thompson Seedless, cherry-red Cardinals, flame-red Tokays, light red to red-purple Emperors, purple-black Ribiers, greenish-white Almerias and Calmerias. Keep them cold and humid and eat within a week.

GREENS: There are many kinds, such as collards, turnip tops, mustard greens, kale, Swiss chard, beet greens, dandelions, cabbage sprouts, broccoli rab, and others. (Spinach is dealt with under its name.) Best quality greens of any kind are fresh, young, tender, and green. They should not show insect injury, coarse stems, seed stems, dry or yellowing leaves, dirt or poor development. They should be crisp, never wilted or flabby. They need to be cold and moist at all times. Greens that are warm when sold should be suspect. Use as soon as possible. Greens of one kind or another are on the market all year.

GUAVAS: This subtropical fruit is cultivated to a small extent in Florida. In fresh form it is very scarce. The fruit may be round, oval, oblong, or pear-shaped, one to four inches in diameter, with a thin skin green to bright yellow with sometimes a pink blush. When fully ripe it is sweet and only mildly acidic. Most of the guavas are processed into preserves and jellies. Keep cool and humid and use as soon as possible.

HONEYDEWS: This is a smooth greenish-white-skinned, large, green-fleshed variety of muskmelon. It is difficult to know whether a fruit offered for sale is mature. In general, a creamy color and velvety surface shows ripeness, but color can vary with origin. Usually melons, if they have a green color, are unripe. Such melons will not sweeten and will be unsatisfactory. The rind of a ripe melon has a soft and velvety feel. Honeydews have best flavor when served at room temperature. Unless they are ripe, hold them at room temperature a couple of days before serving. When ripe, keep cool and humid if they are to be kept longer. They are available February through October but mostly in March and June through October.

HORSERADISH ROOT: Look for firm roots with no soft spots or shriveling. Keep cold and humid and use as desired. Roots dug when the plant is still growing do not keep as well as those conditioned by cold weather before harvest. Available all year in some markets.

JERUSALEM ARTICHOKES: This vegetable is not an artichoke and has nothing to do with Jerusalem. It is related to the sunflower. The tubers that vary to three inches in diameter are the plant part that is eaten. The tubers shrivel readily when exposed to air, so they should be kept in a plastic bag and refrigerated. Planting is irregular and the marketing season and supply uncertain.

KIWI: Fuzzy, small cylindrical fruits from New Zealand. They should be somewhat firm when bought. When ripe they yield to gentle pressure. After ripening, if not used immediately, refrigerate and serve within a day or two. Available June to December.

KOHLRABI: This member of the cabbage family has a stem swollen just above the ground into a globe three or four inches in diameter. The leaves are similar to those of a turnip. When young, both bulb and leaves can be eaten after being boiled or steamed. The bulb should be firm and crisp and not too large. It may be eaten raw. The tops should be crisp and green. Keep cold and use within a few days. Available May through November with peak in June and July, but supply is always small.

KUMQUATS: This is a decorative holiday fruit, the smallest of the citrus group. The fruits usually are orange-colored, oblong, 1¼ by 1½ inches, and often are marketed with some leaves. They make a fine display and are edible. They may be kept at room temperature or refrigerated. The marketing period is November into March.

LEEKS: Leeks of good quality have green, fresh tops and medium-size necks that are well blanched for at least two or three inches from the root and that are young, crisp, and tender. Yellowed, wilted, or otherwise damaged tops may indicate old age and flabby, tough, and fibrous necks. Slight bruising of the tops is not important. Leeks are usually milder than green onions. Keep them cold and humid and use within a week or so. Available all year in small supply, with peak September through November and in the spring.

LEMONS: They should have a rich yellow color, fine textured skin, be heavy for their size, and be moderately firm. These points are indications of juiciness. They need not be refrigerated for the first few days to a week. Available all year in large amounts.

LETTUCE: There are various kinds of lettuce, even some with red leaves, but the main type is the solid-headed kind generally called iceberg. Good quality iceberg should be clean, crisp, tender with firm heads, free from seed stems and leaves with ragged brown areas. Butterhead, Boston, romaine, Bibb, and loose-leaf lettuce should be clean, fresh, and tender. All kinds should be kept cold and humid and used within a few days. Iceberg is available all year in large amounts and the others in smaller and less certain supplies.

LIMES: Domestic limes should be bright green and heavy for their size. Yellow fruit lacks acidity. Fruit with purple to brown irregular-shaped spots is affected with scald and is undesirable. The Mexican, or key lime, is light yellow when ripe and is an exception to the "buy them green" rule. They may be kept at room temperature for the few days likely to elapse before use. They are available all year with peak June through August.

LITCHIS: The litchi fruit is from a subtropical tree native to South China and cultivated in Florida. The fruits are round to oval, one to one and a half inches in diameter, with a bright red leathery skin with small conical protuberances. The edible portion is the translucent white to pale cream covering of the seed, with about the same consistency as a fresh grape. It has a slightly interesting acid flavor. Refrigerate and use as soon as possible. The bulk of the Florida crop matures between mid-June and early July and is marketed as maturity permits.

MANGOES: This tropical fruit normally has a smooth outer skin, usually green with yellowish to red areas. It is round to oval, varying considerably in size, weighing from half a pound to a pound. The red and yellow increases as the fruit ripens. The pulp is yellow, delicate, juicy, and has a flavor that reminds one of apricot and pineapple, but when unripe of turpentine. Reject mangoes that are wilted or have grayish discoloration of the skin or pitting or black spots, or any sign of decay. At home, keep them at room temperature until very soft, and then eat as soon as possible. When fully soft, refrigerate. They are available mostly May through August.

MUSHROOMS: Only one species is cultivated in this country and that is *Agaricus campestris,* the common field mushroom modified in cultivation. The flesh is firm, thick, and white. They should be clean, fresh in appearance, white to creamy white, free from pitting, discoloration, wilting or other injury, and have closed caps. Sizes ranging from three-fourths of an inch to three inches in diameter are usually preferred. If mushroom caps are partially open, the gills (fluted formation between cap and stem) should be light in color. Brown or black gills indicate old age. Keep cold and humid and use as soon as possible. On market all year with peak period November through April.

NECTARINES: Look for smooth, plump, brightly colored, unblemished fruit. Like the peach, the nectarine does not gain sugar after harvest and must be picked well matured to be satisfactory. Mature fruit will soften and become juicy. Fruit with considerable green is likely to be unsatisfactory. Avoid hard, dull fruits and any that show shriveling, a sign of immaturity. Give them plenty of time to soften. When soft, keep cold and humid and use as soon as possible. Available mostly June into September.

OKRA: Pods should be young, tender, fresh, clean, and preferably of medium size, two to four inches long. They should snap easily when broken and be easily punctured, which indicates tenderness. Dull, dry pods will be unpalatable; and shriveled or discolored pods lack flavor. Keep cool and humid and use as soon as possible. On the market mostly from May into October.

ONIONS, DRY: They should be bright, clean, hard, well shaped, with dry skins that crackle. A thick, tough, woody, or open condition of the neck or presence of a stem indicates seed-stem development. Shape is not too important except that for some uses there may be excessive waste in preparation of off-shape bulbs such as splits, doubles, and bottlenecks. Moisture at the neck is an indication of decay. They may be refrigerated or kept at room temperature, but keep them dry. On the market all year in large amounts. Neither color, size, nor shape indicates pungency; however, Bermuda and red Italian onions are sweeter.

ONIONS, GREEN: A green onion is small, elongated, with an edible green stem; it is milder than any onion, except chives. There are a number of types, but all should have green, fresh tops, medium-size stems, and be well blanched for several inches from the root, and should be young, crisp, and tender. Wilted or discolored tops indicate poor quality. Keep cold and humid and use as soon as possible. They are on the market all year with more May through August. Green onions are frequently called scallions.

ORANGES: Oranges of the best quality are firm, heavy, have a fine-textured skin, varying, however, according to variety, and have few or no seeds. The seedier the orange, of course, the less edible pulp and juice there is. Color at destination is of no value in judging the maturity of the fruit. All oranges, as required by law, are picked mature, depending on color and their acid and soluble solids content. Green fruit is as ripe as golden fruit and in fact sometimes fruit picked all golden turns green. Florida oranges may have color added to satisfy the public view that an orange is supposed to be orange-colored. Such fruit is stamped "color added." The color is harmless. Avoid oranges that are light, puffy, or spongy, since they lack juice. Oranges may be kept at room temperature or kept cold and may be used as desired. They are available all year, with largest supplies December into May.

PAPAYAS: Papayas of moderate size, but bigger than a large pear are usually preferred. Very large fruit may not have as much flavor as the medium sizes. Select fruit that is well colored, that is, at least half yellowish and with no large amount of green. The skin should be smooth, unbruised, unbroken, showing no signs of deterioration or shriveling. The shape of the fruit should be something like that of a pear. If not ripe, that is, yellow and yielding to slight pressure between the palms, ripen at room temperature, then refrigerate and use as soon as possible. On market all year in small amounts, with peak in May and June.

PARSLEY: Parsley should be bright, fresh, green, crisp, and free from yellow leaves or dirt. Wilting and yellowing mean old age or damage. Keep cold and humid and use as desired. There is an advantage in storing parsley with stems in water, or in a tightly covered jar. Parsley root, which is sold separately, keeps well when cold and humid. On the market all year.

PARSNIPS: Parsnip flavor is not fully developed until after prolonged exposure to temperatures around 40° F or lower. Parsnips should have been stored, not come direct from the field. They should be smooth, firm, clean, well-shaped, of small to medium size. Soft, flabby, or shriveled roots are pithy or fibrous. Softness may also be an indication of decay. Large, coarse parsnips are apt to have tough, woody cores. Discoloration may be an indication of freezing. Keep cold and humid and use as desired. They are on the market mostly October through April.

PEACHES: The first rule of peach buying is to insist on mature peaches only, no green ones. A peach does not gain sugar after picking since it has no starch to convert to sugar, so it is desirable to obtain peaches as near tree-ripe as possible. Full tree-ripeness is not commercially feasible because of damage in marketing. Fruit picked green does not ripen; it merely shrivels. Hydrocooled fruit is preferable, since it can be picked nearer the ripe stage if given an ice-cold bath soon after harvest. Maturity is indicated by yellowish color and red blush and general absence of greenness. Hold peaches at room temperature until soft enough to eat, then refrigerate and use as soon as possible. If any sign of brown rot developes, use at once because it works fast. They are on the market mostly June through September.

PEARS: In western commerical areas, pears are picked mature but hard, and they reach ideal ripeness off the trees. A "tree-ripened" pear would be much inferior and no such pears are offered by professional growers. Buy pears of standard varieties that are firm, free from blemishes, and clean, not misshapen, wilted, or shriveled. In general, big, plump pears are the best. The Bartlett is yellow with a red blush when ripe, but note that Anjous are still green or greenish yellow when ripe, Cormice is green, and the Bosc dark yellow overlaid with cinnamon-russet. Ripen pears at room temperature, but if purchased in a plastic bag, open the bag a little. The main problem with pears is to tell when they are ripe. They ripen from inside out and should not be held until soft on the outside. At that stage, the inside may be too soft. Eat pears while still firm but not hard. Bartlett pears develop a delightful perfume when ready to eat. When ripe, keep cold and humid and eat as soon as possible. On market mainly August through March.

PEAS, GREEN: Fresh green peas are rarely seen on the market anymore since fresh peas of high quality are difficult to find. This is because they must be young to be good, and must be cooled quickly after harvest and kept cold; they lose sugar—and tenderness—quickly. Pods should be uniformly green and well filled. Use as soon as possible. They are on the market April through July. Home grown peas are by far the best.

PEPPERS, SWEET: Bell peppers should be fresh, firm, bright, thick-fleshed, and either bright green or red. Immature peppers are usually soft and dull-looking. The kinds most used are four to five inches long, are three- or four-lobed, and taper only slightly toward the blossom end. Keep cool and humid and use within a few days. They are on the market all year with more May through October.

PERSIANS: This muskmelon is globe-shaped and averages about seven and one-half inches in diameter with weight about seven pounds. The rind is dark green covered with a fine netting, and the flesh is orange and very thick. As they ripen, the rind under the netting turns a lighter green and gives under light pressure. They do not gain sugar after harvesting but will soften and become juicy. Give them time for these changes. After softening, keep cold and humid and use as soon as possible. Their season is mostly July into October.

PERSIMMONS: The Oriental or Japanese persimmon, grown in California, is larger than a large plum, oblong-conic, with a rounded apex. The green cap should be in place. It is bright orange and seedless. Make sure the fruit is plump with smooth, highly colored skin, and no damage. Keep at room temperature until it is as soft as jelly. At this stage it has a rich and sweet flavor. When ripe, keep cold and humid and use as soon as possible. In season mostly October through December.

PINEAPPLES: Select fruit heavy for its size and as large as

possible. The larger the fruit, the greater the proportion of edible flesh. Look for freshness and especially crown leaves that are fresh and deep green. Fruit with brown leaves and other indications of dryness should be rejected. Fragrance is a good sign, but usually the fruit is kept too cold to give off an aroma. Shell color is not an indication of maturity. The grower relies on a test of sugar content but the shopper can't use that. Pulling out crown leaves is not a very reliable test. Avoid pineapples with discolored or soft spots. Do not figure on "ripening" a pineapple even though this is often suggested. Keep cold and humid and use as soon as possible. They are available all year with peak March through June.

PLANTAINS: The plantain is usually thought of as a large, starchy, acidic, and gummy type of banana for cooking, and thought of as not becoming sweet. There are bananas, however, that do not sweeten and plantains that do. Generally speaking, the plantains imported into this country are of the cooking type and should be cooked before reaching full ripeness. Select as in choosing unripe bananas. Small amounts of plantains are available all year in some areas.

PLUMS AND ITALIAN PRUNES: Plums and fresh prunes of good quality are plump, clean, fresh-looking, full colored for the variety, and not hard. They should at least be beginning to soften when displayed at the retail market. They must be picked firm, however, or they could not survive the marketing period. If picked mature with adequate sugar content, they need only be allowed to soften at room temperature. Sometimes this takes three or four days. Many persons are disappointed with plums because they do not give them enough time to soften and become juicy. But hard, immature plums will not ripen properly. It is difficult to tell such plums by color unless you know the characteristic color of the variety when ripe. Some plums are ripe when yellowish green, others, such as Italian prunes, when purplish black, with many colors in between. After ripening, keep cold and humid and use as soon as possible. They are on the market mainly June into September.

POMEGRANATES: The pomegranate is about the size of an apple, has a thin, tough rind that should be pink or bright red, and the flesh is crimson. They have a large number of small seeds each surrounded by juicy pulp with a spicy taste. Reject any that look hard and dry. Keep cold and humid until used. They are on the market from late September into November, with two-thirds of the annual total in October.

POTATOES: Potatoes of any kind or size should be firm, relatively smooth, clean, reasonably well shaped, not badly cut or bruised or skinned, nor should they show any green from light-burn. They should not be wilted or show sprouts. Cooking quality varies by variety and production areas. Aside from size, some types from some areas, such as Idaho and Colorado, are known to be good bakers. This is because of their high content of dry matter. Do not refrigerate. In most households it is practical to keep potatoes at room temperature but in the dark and away from hot pipes or radiators or places where they could become too cold. They are on the market all year in large amounts.

PUMPKINS: Selection depends on whether the pumpkin is for eating or scaring people. In any event, aside from size, the pumpkin should be of good orange-golden color, have a hard rind, heavy in relation to size, and be free from cuts or severe bruises. Keep cool until ready to use. Available mostly in October.

RADISHES: There are various types such as globular red and white, globular white, long red, long white, and long black. They should all be fresh, well formed, smooth, firm, crisp, and not showing any cuts, black spots, or pits. Pithy, spongy, or wilted radishes are undesirable. Most of them now come topped and bagged, but if tops are on, they should be fresh and green. Such tops can be cooked and eaten. Keep the roots cold and humid. Radishes are on the market in good quantities all year, with more May through July.

RHUBARB: Good quality rhubarb stalks are fresh, firm, crisp, tender, and bright in appearance. Stalks should not be excessively thin. Stalks with considerable red are usually more flavorful, but some varieties from some soils have little red and yet have good flavor. The younger stems, having immature leaves, are the most tender and delicate in flavor. (Do not eat any leaves.) Wilted or flabby stalks indicate stringiness, lack of freshness, and poor flavor. Oversize stalks may be tough. Tenderness and crispness can be tested by puncturing the stalk. Keep cold and humid and use as desired. Rhubarb is on the market mostly January through June.

RUTABAGAS: Virtually all rutabagas are yellow-fleshed, distinguishing them in a general way from turnips, which are mostly white-fleshed. Rutabagas are also higher in total dry matter and total digestible nutrients than turnips; and rutabagas are slightly more elongated than turnips and have a thick neck. Rutabagas should be firm, fresh-looking, heavy for their size, generally smooth, not deeply cut or punctured, and not showing any decay. Size is not a quality factor. Keep them cold and humid and use as desired. Rutabagas are on the market all year but more are available in the cold months.

SHALLOTS: They are distinguished from onions by the bulb made up of individual cloves like garlic. Shallots of good quality have green fresh tops and medium-size necks that are well blanched for at least two or three inches from the root. Keep them cold and humid. They are available in fresh form mainly November through April. Dried shallots are quite satisfactory and available all year.

SPINACH: The leaves should be clean, fresh, tender, and of a dark green color. Small, lighter-green undeveloped heart leaves are not objectionable, but larger leaves that are yellow, discolored, wilted, bruised, or crushed are unacceptable. If in the form of plants, the spinach should be well developed and relatively stocky. Straggly, over-grown plants or plants with seed stems are undesirable. Most spinach is of the savory or crumpled-leaf type, but whether savory or smooth is not important. It is very perishable, so keep it cold and humid and use as soon as possible. Fresh spinach is on the market all year, with more January through May.

SQUASH: Squashes are conveniently grouped into (1) soft-skinned, immature, and small; (2) hard-shelled, mature, and small; and (3) hard-shelled, mature, and large. The terms "winter" and "summer" squash are confusing and meaningless. The soft-skinned squashes to be eaten skin and all, including seeds, should be young, tender, crisp, fresh, and fairly heavy in relation to size. Tenderness is the main thing for this type of squash. Soft-skinned squashes should be kept cold and humid and used within a few days. On the other hand, the hard-rind type should not have any softness of rind, which would indicate immaturity and thin flesh. The hard-shelled squashes may be kept at room temperature and used as desired, but they cannot be kept a long time under warm conditions. Squashes are on the market all year, with the large hard-shell squashes such as Hubbard on the market in fall and winter.

STRAWBERRIES: Strawberries should be fresh, clean, bright, have solid red color or at least very little white or green, have caps in place, and be free of moisture and mold. Small, misshapen berries usually are of poor texture and flavor, but on the other hand, extremely large berries are likely to lack flavor and be undesirable. Stained containers indicate leakage and spoilage. Strawberries are highly perishable, should be kept cold and humid, and should be used as soon as possible. They are available all year but peak April through June.

SWEET POTATOES: They should be clean, smooth, well shaped, firm, and bright in appearance with good coloring according to type. Some have copper-colored skin, others lighter-tan skin. Whether yellow-fleshed or orange-fleshed tubers are chosen is a matter of individual choice. The copper-skinned kinds with orange flesh are softer, the yellow-fleshed type generally firmer. Keep sweet potatoes dry and do not refrigerate. Cold is harmful to sweet potatoes. They are on the market all year but much more October through April.

TANGELOS: Like other citrus, quality is determined at the grove by tests of acids and soluble solids, not external appearance alone. The best fruit, however, is firm, heavy for its size, thin-skinned, with light-orange peel, and not badly blemished. Tangelos are hybrids of mandarin oranges and grapefruit. They have an excellent taste all their own. They may be kept at room temperature or kept cold and humid, depending on length of storage. They are on the market from late October through January.

TANGERINES: They should be heavy for their size, indicating ample juice, and have the characteristic deep orange or almost red color. A puffy appearance and feel is normal, since the skin zips off, but there should not be any soft or water-soaked areas. They are highly perishable. Keep them cold and humid and use as soon as possible. On the market mainly November through January.

TOMATOES: Tomatoes picked with any degree of pinkness (so-called vine-ripe) can attain good taste and texture if properly handled. It is not necessary that a tomato be 100 percent red when offered at retail. It has been found that many consumers prefer the taste of a tomato with some green. Tomatoes are quite a problem for the consumer, because even a tomato picked immature green will redden 100 percent, though it will not necessarily attain good flavor and juiciness. Furthermore, a tomato, even though picked pink or red, shipped at too cold a temperature will chill and then not ripen properly. It is not possible, therefore, to give the shopper a formula for tomato selection. It appears necessary to find a retailer who regularly stocks tomatoes that turn out to be good, then pick out those of the desired size and color and that are not too ripe. Ideally, tomatoes come from garden to table. At home, keep tomatoes at room temperature in the open until they are at the stage desired. They are on the market all year; best in summer and fall.

TURNIPS: Turnips differ in shape and skin color, but different varieties have much the same flavor. Most turnips are white-fleshed. They should be smooth, firm, and with few leaf scars around the crown or fibrous roots at the base. If tops are on, they should be fresh, green and crisp. Yellowed or wilted tops indicate old age. Roots that are very large and coarse or that are in any degree wilted should be rejected. If tops are on and good enough to eat, they should be removed and used as soon as possible. Topped turnips should be kept cold and humid and used as desired. They are available all year.

UGLIFRUIT: This fruit, possibly a form of tangelo, lives up to its name. It has an extremely rough peel commonly disfigured with blemishes. When mature it has an orange color with blotches of light green. It's a specialty fruit for people who like the unusual. It has one to six seeds and eleven sections, and is very juicy with an interesting orangelike flavor. It need not be refrigerated. The marketing season is winter.

WATERMELONS: The essential factors of watermelon quality are maturity and size. The larger melons have more edible flesh, proportionately to weight, than the smaller ones. Maturity is difficult to determine without plugging and testing. Usually, ripe melons of good quality are firm, symmetrical, fresh-looking with an attractive waxy bloom, and with good characteristic color for the variety. The lower side should be somewhat yellowish where the melon contacted the soil. If a melon is very hard and is white or very pale green on the under side it is probably immature. If so, don't undertake to ripen it; in the watermelon, total sugar does not increase after it comes off the vine. Thumping a melon can provide exercise, but not much else for anyone other than a watermelon expert. Better look for a typical melon the retailer has cut and then you can know what his melons look like inside. They should have red flesh and black seeds. At home they may be kept at room temperature until cut or may be refrigerated. On market mostly May into September.

WATERCRESS: It should be fresh, young, crisp, tender, rich medium-green, and free from dirt or yellowed leaves.

Wilting or discoloration indicates old age. There is only one variety of true watercress—with accent on the "water"—but there are other cresses that grow wild in marshy areas and there are also land cresses. As with other leafy greens, keep cold and wet. It is highly perishable, so use it as soon as possible. Enclosing it in a film bag with ice or a little cold water is a good practice. On the market all year in small amounts.

What Is "Organic?"

Buyers of fresh fruits and vegetables often see the term *organic* used to describe some produce. Or the term used is *organically grown* commodities, which the sellers allege have been grown without use of chemical fertilizers or chemical pesticides. They say that these are "healthier" and some claim they are more "nutritious."

All plants use inorganic, not organic nutrients. The reasons are that plants must have nutrients dissolved in water, while organic substances require other solvents; and that plants absorb minerals in the form of ions, that is, electrically charged particles, which provide fast reactions, while organic compounds are mostly uncharged and have slow reactions. If a plant is given nothing but organic fertilizers from farm animals, it is necessary for soil organisms to break down the organic molecules to inorganic forms before they are used.

This is no indictment of organic fertilizers. They are useful in promoting retention of water, preventing caking, increasing porosity and aeration of soil, and providing material that can be broken down into forms the plant can use. But to allege that a fruit or vegetable from a plant fertilized organically is superior nutritionally to products fertilized with chemicals (bearing in mind that organic fertilizer is also chemicals) is just plain bunk. Tests have been made by the U.S. Department of Agriculture and by universities and they show the nutritional value of a plant is similar whether from soil fertilized organically or inorganically, or neither.

Why, then, is an orange high in ascorbic acid but not vitamin A and a carrot high in vitamin A and not in ascorbic acid? The reason lies in the answer to the basic question, Why does one seed grow into a carrot and another into an orange tree? The answer is the difference in genes. That is also the answer to the question of why products from two different kinds of plants differ so much in composition. The difference is primarily genetic. No amount of any kind of fertilizers changes the plant genes and so oranges and carrots will continue to be different and fertilizers will not change their basic composition, though they will change the size and quality of the crop.

Almost all the fruits and vegetables in the United States are grown scientifically with the use of the chemical fertilizers that are necessary for each kind of plant and each kind of soil; and with such application of chemicals as is necessary to control pests so that enough food can be raised to feed our 200 million people.

Preparing Fruits and Vegetables for Salads

Nothing looks better on a salad than fresh fruits and vegetables that have been cut, diced, shredded, or shaped into a variety of sizes, creating interesting shapes and textures. Very few fruits or vegetables are served whole. The exceptions are seedless grapes, cherry tomatoes, mushrooms, tiny cooked beets, peas and string beans. Those fruits and vegetables add color and fun to a salad and will still blend well with the other ingredients.

In order to create a good blending of flavors and ingredients and to make foods easier to eat, it is often necessary to prepare some fruits and vegetables by cutting and slicing. You can chop, slice, grate, shave, peel, shred or score; the method you use will be dictated by the look and texture of the food itself.

Utensils

Electric food processors are invaluable for slicing or grating raw vegetables. They work incredibly fast, but remember: when chopping, turn on the machine for only a moment at a time and watch closely to be sure the result will not be too fine.

Blenders, which do not slice, also cut up vegetables very fast. They should be run at their lowest speed and checked frequently—unless you want purée.

Hand-run slicers, choppers and *graters* are available with easy-to-follow instructions. But one can get along with a vegetable scraper, a sharp, medium-size kitchen knife, a solid chopping board, and careful attention to keeping the sizes of the vegetables uniform.

Shaping Vegetables

As a rule, fresh vegetables need only to be washed or scrubbed before slicing. Tough skins are easily shaved off with a knife or vegetable scraper.

Avocados make excellent containers when cut in half. The pit is removed and the skin left on; scoop out some of the flesh with a spoon and then fill the hole. The skin of an avocado needs to be removed when it is sliced. Avocado slices make a delicious garnish, while chunks of avocado add real flavor to a green salad.

Beets, which are not used raw, are among the vegetables that do taste good canned. If you cook them yourself, leave a bit of the stem on them so they won't bleed, and rub off the outer skin after they are boiled; then slice, dice, or julienne. NOTE: Julienne vegetables are long strips about the size of wooden matches made from raw or cooked vegetables.

Cabbage for slaw should be sliced, shredded, or chopped.

Carrots are very versatile. They can be shaved into curls with a vegetable scraper (fasten the curls with toothpicks and store in the refrigerator in ice water). Hand-grated, they make an excellent color addition to a green salad, or they can be sliced or cut into julienne strips.

Cauliflower, whether cooked or raw, is most attractive when separated into flowerettes, although it can also be sliced.

Celery is one of the most popular fresh vegetables today. Besides being almost calorie-free, eating celery is actually good for your teeth—strengthening and cleaning them. Pull the celery stalks apart, scrape or cut off the "strings," and slice across the rib or stalk.

Cucumbers, whether peeled or not, look better when they are sliced if you first score them by running the tines of a fork on them from top to bottom. The slices will have small indentations around the edges, giving them a petallike appearance. Cucumbers can also be cut lengthwise into long or finger-length strips; or they can be seeded and chopped. Seed cucumbers by running a sharp knife under the row of seeds.

Garlic is strong, and should be minced as fine as possible after the dry skin surrounding each segment or clove has been removed. A garlic press is very useful in obtaining juicy crushed garlic.

Green beans, unless they are very young, crisp, and tender, should be cooked. They must have their tips removed and then can be left whole, cut lengthwise, across, or on the slant (the latter being called *french cut*).

Mushrooms are often served whole. But when they are too large to be eaten whole they can be cut through the crown and stem, or sliced into pieces, or the stem and crown can be cut separately. If discolored, they can be peeled.

Onions may be cut in half and placed facedown before chopping. The strength of an onion should determine the size of its pieces. Generous rounds of Bermuda onions are acceptable, while anything more than slivers of white globe onions would be too much. Scallions can be served whole or can be chopped and added to a salad. Slice or mince the green part as well as the pale end.

Peppers are not skinned. After the seeds and white pulp have been removed, cut them into circular strips or lengthwise slices; or chop them into large or small cubes.

Potatoes may be peeled and sliced or diced while they are still warm.

Radishes can be made into decorative flowers by cutting half-a-dozen petals from the top almost to the bottom. They also look attractive when they are sliced—skin and all—into thin rounds.

Delicious and Decorative Fruits

Apples can be used with or without the peel. They can be sliced, cubed, or cut into segments.

Bananas can be sliced, cubed, or split.

Berries and small fruits are left whole, although the pits must be removed from cherries and plums before serving.

Citrus fruits must be peeled with a knife sharp enough to remove all the skin and white membrane, or they can be cut into slices with the peel on or off for garnish.

Grapes can be used whole with or without seeds.

Melons may be halved and used as containers. Peeled melons can be sliced or cubed, melon balls can be made with a special scoop or cutter.

Peaches can be peeled and then pitted easily once the fruit is cut in half.

Pears can be sliced, chopped, or sectioned after the seeds and the skin have been removed. If sections are cut almost to the bottom, the lower section should be retained intact. If the fruits are halved lengthwise, they can be used as containers for cottage cheese or other fillings.

Pineapple is peeled and the flesh is cut into fingers, slices, cubes, or fancy shapes. Some of the flesh may be scooped out of the pineapple and the halves with the spiky leaves left on can be used as containers. Using frozen melon and pineapple shells for containers is described in the "Serving Your Salad" section.

NOTE: Remember, a sprinkle of lemon juice over avocados, apples and bananas keeps them from browning.

Texture Your Salad

Texture is as important as taste. Everyone knows how monotonous a bland diet soon becomes, and how quickly we weary when an entire meal is "chewy." Just as a crisp cookie makes ice cream more enjoyable, and toasted almonds compliment a soft fish, crisp and crunchy salads, such as cole slaw, or hearts of iceberg lettuce, perk up noodle casseroles and ham or cheese soufflés, while a smooth aspic or tender greens provide a pleasant contrast to crusty dishes such as southern fried chicken. Contrasts within a salad bowl are equally welcome. A few suggestions that add contrast as well as flavor are:

- crisp bacon bits on sliced avocado
- celery with tuna fish
- hard onion slices on marinated (limp) cucumbers
- slivered ham on soft Boston lettuce
- grapefruit sections or beets on Belgian endive
- yogurt on raw spinach
- croutons on tossed greens
- kidney beans on shredded iceberg lettuce
- crisp chopped scallions on sliced tomatoes

We need not turn to harsh brans for bulk in our diet. In addition to the pleasure we get from a variety of textures in a salad, we also benefit because the fibers found in many salads can provide the needed roughage for a healthy digestive system.

Color in Your Salad

Seeing comes before tasting and everyone knows the influence a luscious-looking dish can have on the appetite. Salads offer limitless opportunities to please the eye because they provide an entire spectrum of colors from which to choose. We can have contrasts within the salad itself—such as dark green spinach and creamy white mushrooms or bright red tomatoes and brilliant green beans—and contrasts between the salad and the main dish—ham with potato salad, or beets with chicken. We can have harmony within a salad—cream cheese, grapefruit, and orange on pale lettuce, all cool shades of green to gold, or a bowl of greens shading from the palest endive to the darkest watercress—and a salad that harmonizes with the entrée, cucumbers and fish, for example. Here are a few suggestions for color combinations:

• tomatoes topped with minced basil
• asparagus and red pimiento
• carrots and raisins
• dark greens with bean sprouts

Almost any combination of mixed cooked vegetables provides a variety of colors. Similarly, almost any combination of fruits is attractive; strawberries and pineapple go well together, and so do balls made of vari-colored melons. Jewel-like fruit colors can be enhanced in many ways:

- a sprinkling a grated orange or lemon peel
- cut-up dates sprinkled over other fruits
- dark cherries stuffed with cream cheese
- mint leaves

But it is the platter salad that provides us with the greatest opportunity to create a work of art! We have a palette to work with that will appeal to the eye as well as the taste. Here is a general chart of the array of colors found in nature's kitchen:

RED:	apple, beet, cranberry, pepper, tomato, pimiento
PINK:	peach, pink grapefruit, salmon, shrimp
ORANGE:	salmon roe, carrots, orange, tangerine, Cheddar cheese.
YELLOW:	egg yolks, grapefruit, pineapple
GREEN:	artichoke, asparagus, beans, cucumbers, lettuce, spinach
PURPLE:	cherries, plums, raspberries, eggplants, purple broccoli
BLACK:	capers, caraway, caviar, ripe olives, poppy seeds
WHITE:	white cheeses, chicken, egg white, fish, pears, Belgian endive

Don't forget your salad dressings! They can provide the color itself or can be sprinkled with color. Vinaigrettes can be brightened with chives, grated carrots, peppers, beets, pickles, egg yolks, while mayonnaises can use many of these. Chili sauce. ketchup, curry, and mustard will add zest as well as color to your salad.

Crunchies

Greens tend to be chewy, and they are usually ground in the mouth using the molars. To play up this texture, hard, crisp, and brittle-textured food, or bouncy food are mixed in the salad. Vegetables themselves can be combined to provide variety. Raw vegetables—crudites—make ideal between-meal snacks and appetizers. These crunchies are appropriate for a bedtime snack, also. Attractively cut up into bite-size pieces, or sticks, they store very well in the refrigerator. You can keep an assortment in plastic bags or each kind in its own container for easy selection. Choose from:

- green or red peppers, seeded and cut up
- carrots (young, small whole, or scraped and cut into sticks)
- young green beans with the ends trimmed off
- white or red radishes, scraped (or with the ends cut off or made into roses)
- thin green asparagus, scraped
- cauliflowerettes
- mushrooms
- leaves of Belgian endives or center leaves of garden lettuce
- sprigs of watercress
- very young turnips, scraped and sliced
- cucumbers cut into finger lengths
- scallions, trimmed

- young zucchini (not peeled), cut into finger lengths or rounds
- kohlrabi, peeled and cut into rounds
- snow peas, ends trimmed

You may have on hand seasoned salt or a dip, if you wish. Other salad texturizers are:

- sunflower and pumpkin seeds
- raisins
- nuts such as cashews, almonds, filberts, pecans, walnuts, or peanuts
- dried fruit such as prunes, apples, apricots, peaches, figs, and dates
- bite-size pieces of firm cheeses.

In the summer, a large variety of fruits and vegetables is available. This is the season when they are at their most flavorful, and also the texture is often at it's best—from hard and crispy to sweet and soft.

Serving Your Salad

The presentation of a salad should be worthy of the skill and care that has gone into its preparation. That doesn't mean it has to be fancy; nothing is more attractive than the sight of simple greens being tossed in a wooden bowl. Do not waste your time making complicated garnishes. Please the eye by blending and contrasting colors, and through the use of attractive garnishes.

When serving salads in a large container, whether it is a bowl or platter, the picture, as a whole, is important. When the salad is served in individual portions, think in terms of vignettes. Appetizers and side salads are generally placed on the table in individual bowls or on plates before the guests are seated. Salad appetizers are centered on the service plates; side salads are on the left of the table settings. The dishes need not match the rest of the china and can be almost any type or design—wood, glass, pottery, china, or stainless steel; plates, bowls, platters, or even seashells. It is best to avoid silver because it is quickly discolored by salad dressing. Salads can be dressed ahead of time, or the dressing can be passed around in any decorative container, from a gravy boat to a small pitcher.

Not only greens, but heavy mixed salads can be served from large containers that are round, oval, deep, or shallow. Deep bowls are best for leafy salads that would easily drop off of a flat plate.

Aspics look their jewel-like best set on a flat surface.

Three-dimensional or flowerlike salads, such as an arti-choke or a tomato "cup" or a mound of salmon sur-rounded by overlapping slices of cucumbers, or peach halves filled with cottage cheese, also are best on a flat plate.

Nothing is more becoming to a fruit salad than clear crystal through which the beautiful colors can easily be seen.

A salad bar can offer containers of all types and sizes including small servers for the salad dressings and gar-nishes. When presenting a rainbow-hued platter salad on your most elegant plate, leave a little space between the various ingredients so that the guests don't ruin your picture when helping themselves.

In addition to all the materials at your disposal, you can make your own dessert salad bowls by scooping the flesh out of melon, oranges, or pineapple halves and using the shells. If you freeze them before using, no juice will seep out and your salad will stay cool longer; and after a quick rinse, your "bowl" can be refrozen for another occasion. If you are using pineapple for your bowl, cut lengthwise through the stem and leaves; if you're using melons, you can "pink" the edges with a sharp knife.

Traditionally, salad is served using a large, long-handled spoon and fork. You can use any graceful or handy service utensil from tongs to a spatula.

Salads in Entertaining

A "company meal," whether formal or informal, simple or elegant, requires a salad. It can be a light one to whet the appetite, a salad made of greens to clear the palate, an unusual combination to furnish a topic of conversation, or a beautiful composition of carefully cut vegetables and fruits, but it must be *there*, for party time is the time of salads.

When giving an elegant dinner, produce the new salad you have been saving for a special occasion; new to your guests, that is, but not entirely new to you—better try it ahead of time. This usually calls for an extra expenditure of time or money or both. Extravagances such as hearts of palm, artichoke bottoms, or Belgian endive will make a meal memorable. If you would rather spend time than money, prepare a handsome aspic with a variety of chopped or slivered raw vegetables or cut-up fruits. A salad made of equal parts of thinly sliced mushrooms and scraped celery slivers is worth the time it takes. The presentation of the salad is most important.

The Salad Bar

A new and exciting way to entertaining is the salad bar, which has moved from the restaurant to the home. The ingredients for the salads are attractively displayed in individual dishes so that the guests can choose to suit their own tastes and diets. For the hostess, this convivial touch, which the salad bar gives to rather formal dinners, relieves her, or a helper, from having a course to serve. Since the guests serve themselves, the bar should offer a variety of dishes from which to choose, but an overwhelming number is not necessary or good.

On the salad bar, tossed greens are a must, a big bowl of them. They need no dressing, since each person will choose from the several that are offered. The quantity depends upon the number of persons to be served. Count on at least one cup of tightly packed assorted greens for each portion. They may be chosen from iceberg, Boston, Bibb, escarole, endive (curly or Belgian), leaf, romaine, red, Chinese cabbage, young spinach, and watercress.

Also have several cooked and raw vegetables, such as beets, cucumbers, green peppers, tomatoes, onions, carrots, and zucchini, with three or four garnishes to choose from: grated or diced cheese, croutons, olives, bacon bits, grape nuts, and chopped chives. There must be a choice of dressings: a light French or Italian and several heartier ones such as russian, Roquefort, and mayonnaise, plain, herbed, or with mustard (see page 206).

Portable Salads

In the past, when salads traveled to picnics and to school lunches, they were usually in the form of sandwiches: chicken salad, tuna salad, or egg salad. Now salads are on their own, accompanying sandwiches or even replacing them, and the number and variety has grown accordingly. Their increased mobility is partly due to the fact that plastic containers have become inexpensive and often free, so there is no longer a worry about losing or discarding them. They protect the delicate types of salad; the hardy ones do very well in plastic bags. Even the most fastidious eater can pack a tidy as well as a refreshing salad to eat in the office. They may be packed in paper cups, plastic jars or cartons, or other containers.

For salads that make a long hot-weather trip to eat on a boat, on a tour, perhaps in a camper, you can buy foam plastic hampers and fiberglass-lined tote bags in various sizes. Ice may be placed in them to keep the temperature cool. If you include cubes, place them in a leak-proof plastic bag. The ice is useful for drinks!

For festive picnicking there are English wicker baskets equipped with plates, cups, eating utensils, and food boxes. You don't have to have a fitted basket; you can pack your picnic in a box or shopping bag. Whatever kind of a "to go" meal you are planning, do make it as attractive as possible, including lots of large paper napkins and plastic or coated paper plates.

Salads that should be completed ahead of time, such as cooked vegetable, potato, poultry, shrimp, and even chef's salads, are improved by being marinated en route to their destination. With tender greens, the dressing can be taken in a separate container. Raw vegetables take kindly to being stored in plastic bags with ice, to be eaten as finger food with or without a dip. And, of course, fruit salads are extremely popular with the young of all ages.

For children's parties there are a number of especially appealing ways of serving salads. Easy-to-use utensils include small plastic flowerpots and colorful paper containers of various shapes. Children like salads when they are suited to their taste, and a picnic party is an ideal way of entertaining youngsters.

Here are some events that are perfect for salad takealongs:

office
dieters
special nutrition needs
breaking the "pastry-habit"
cannot leave your deak
visiting
nursery
school

Herbs and Spices

Continents have been discovered and wars have been fought because of herbs and spices. No wonder, since they not only kept some food from spoiling, or made it more palatable when it did spoil, but were considered essential in medicines, religious rituals, in making wine, and even in making love. Conversely, caraway seeds were supposed to prevent infidelity.

No matter how pale a green your thumb may be, you are bound to succeed in growing such herbs as chives, dill, parsley, and mint. A few spices, which come from stems, buds, bark, roots, and seeds, can also be "home grown," but this is much less important, since they are used dried rather than fresh.

There are more than fifty useful herbs and spices. It is wise to become familiar with the most important ones, have some acquaintance with some of the others, and observe a few rules for their use.

The important rule is, Fresh is best. Fresh from your garden, your windowbox or flowerpot, or from your market if you are fortunate enough to have a local grocer or supermarket with a good supply of herbs. Dried or frozen herbs should also be fresh, since they lose their flavor with age. How old is old? Your nose knows, and if you don't trust it, put the date of purchase on each container and get rid of everything that is approaching its first birthday. When you dry or freeze herbs be sure to label as well as date them.

To dry herbs, put them in a slow oven, 200°F or less, for about an hour; a few, such as parsley, take a little longer. They may also be tied in bunches and hung in a dry place—an attic if you have one—for about ten days. Pull the leaves from their stems, crush, and put into tightly covered containers. Pulverize them if you wish, but it is better to do that as you use them. To freeze herbs, plunge them for a few seconds into boiling water and then into ice water. Dry them and freeze in plastic bags or containers. Pull out some as you need them and keep the rest frozen. They will be limp, but quite flavorful.

There are very few occasions when a quarter of a teaspoon of dried herbs won't be enough to flavor a salad for four people. Seasoning to taste really means "tasting to season." Again, speaking generally, one tablespoon of minced fresh herbs is equal to a teaspoon of dried and a half teaspoon of the powdered condiments.

Of course there are some exceptions to this, as to every rule. A tablespoon of fresh dill leaves would not overwhelm a salad of sliced cucumbers; tomatoes can handle quite a lot of fresh basil; and some fruit salads are improved in taste and in appearance by a generous number of sprigs of fresh mint. It is wise, however, to go easy, since it is so much easier to add a little more than it is to take out!

Some herbs are sold in the form of "seasoned" salts. Be sparing if you use these, especially since many people restrict the amount of salt in their diet.

When using dried herbs, put them in the oil or the dressing for at least an hour ahead of time to bring out their flavor.

Remove the leaves of fresh herbs from their tough stems and cut them up with a pair of scissors. They will stay fresh for a day or two in the refrigerator.

Don't use an herb you don't like just because the recipe calls for it. Substitute one you do like. Experiment. Even when you do like an herb, don't stick to it religiously; try thyme or oregano instead of basil on tomatoes, or chervil in place of tarragon on a green salad; a change of herbs can make a familiar salad seem new again. Don't use the same herb twice in one meal.

Use "blended" herbs when it is convenient to do so. *Fines herbes* is a combination of minced parsley and some or all of the following: chervil, chives, basil, or thyme. Curry is a blend of nearly a dozen spices. There's no reason to tackle these oneself when good ones can be purchased ready-made. A good herb farm will know more about blending "salad herbs" than we do, and although each farm has its own variety, most of them are very good and will save a lot of trouble.

Here's to good seasoning!

List of Herbs and Spices

Although *onions* may be regarded as vegetables rather than as herbs (they belong to the lily family), they and their relatives are so important to salads that they deserve a paragraph to themselves. *Chives* are the mildest, *shallots* are stronger, *garlic* the strongest, and *scallions* (green onion) are in between. Onions themselves are of varying strength; Spanish and Bermuda onions are delicate enough to be used, thinly sliced, in some salads, while "regular" globe yellow onions are quite robust. Garlic must always be treated with caution. Rubbing the salad bowl with a cut "clove" (one of the little sections making up the garlic bulb) is usually enough, or let a clove rest for the day in french dressing and then remove it; a few drops of juice from a garlic press is also sufficient.

Thin, tubular green chives are easy to cut over a salad and are delicate enough to be used in almost any salad except desserts. Both the white bottom and the green tops of scallions are good, chopped, when a somewhat stronger flavor is desired. Shallots have a slightly garlicky flavor and should be minced.

BASIL: (*L'herbe royale:* the Greek word for royal is *basil*.) Very aromatic, it is especially good with tomatoes and in french dressing for green salads.

BAY (laurel): Quite strong, it may be used, crushed, in making aspics.

BURNET (the salad herb): Has a slight cucumber flavor; the

tender leaves may be used in vegetable or mixed green salads.

CAPERS: These tiny green flower buds are pickled; good in chicken and meat salads.

CARAWAY SEEDS: Pungent; small quantities are good in slaws and other flavorful salads; good with cabbages or salad that includes cheese.

CARDAMOM: A popular spice in India; good with grapefruit or orange salads.

CELERY SEEDS: Quite flavorful, these tiny seeds may be used whenever the taste rather than the texture of celery is desired.

CHERVIL: Mild, with a resemblance to tarragon and parsley.

CINNAMON: The dried, inner bark of the cassia tree. Ground, it is good in dessert and fruit salads.

CLOVES ("spice nails"): Dried buds, their fragrance and flavor are an addition to fruits and also to pickled mushrooms and cucumbers.

DILL (dillweed): Use the leaves or seeds, the stems are rather bitter. Generally associated with cucumbers and pickles, dill is excellent in slaws, potato salads, and seafood.

FENNEL SEEDS (ground): Slightly resembling licorice and anise, they go well with fish, shellfish, and mixed greens.

GARLIC: Has a strong distinct odor and taste; good with tossed greens.

GINGER (root): May be minced, grated, or ground and used sparingly to add a pungent, sweetish flavor to poultry, seafood, and greens.

MARJORAM (sweet marjoram): Fragrant and less strong than the wild form, which is oregano. Good with poultry, mushrooms, and greens.

MINT: There are many varieties, almost all of which are

good in fruit salads. Very attractive when fresh if used as a garnish.

MUSTARD: Dry or wet (prepared), it adds zest to most salad dressings. Especially good in egg salads.

NUTMEG: Grate a few grains of this seed into fruit and dessert salads.

OREGANO: Very popular in Italy and Spain, it should be used, sparingly, in seafood, mushroom, potato, cheese, and mixed salads.

PAPRIKA: The mildest and sweetest of the red peppers, it adds color as well as flavor to vegetable and fish salads.

PARSLEY: Dark green, mild, and decorative, it enhances all but dessert salads.

PEPPER: The most widely used of spices, needed in most salads, except desserts. White peppercorns are somewhat milder than the black and dark brown, and are better in the paler salads. To obtain the best flavor, pepper should be freshly ground—in the kitchen, at the table, or both.

POPPY SEEDS: These tiny seeds (50,000 to the ounce) are good sprinkled on potato and fruit salads.

ROSEMARY: Quite aromatic, this should be used cautiously in stuffed egg, beef, or spinach salads.

SAFFRON (made from the stigmas of crocuses): It takes an acre of flowers and much labor to make a pound of saffron. Fortunately, a small pinch of it will give an exotic taste and an orange color to rice, fish, and chicken salads.

SAGE: Has a strong, almost astringent flavor; use very sparingly in dips, eggs, fish, and meat salads.

SAVORY (summer savory): It is called the bean herb because of its affinity with the bean family. Used in salads and aspics; also good with tossed greens.

SESAME SEEDS: Especially when toasted, they are recommended for fruit and vegetable salads. They may be crushed to give a stronger flavor.

SORREL (sour grass): Has an acid taste; the fresh, very young leaves give a piquant touch to other greens; especially good with fish.

TARRAGON: Usually pungent, it adds flavor to wine vinegar and also to fish, poultry, asparagus, and other vegetables.

THYME: Fragrant and powerful; small quantities perk up fish, tomatoes, beets, and other vegetables.

Garnishes

Traditionally, garnishes are edible foods that are used to decorate or enhance the look of a dish. Vegetables are wonderful garnishes for all meats, appetizers, and other foods . . . and are natural garnishes for salads. Slicing and dicing to form fruits or vegetables into pretty shapes and then arranging the sliced vegetables on your salad can greatly improve any salad. Carved garnishes are dated. At one time turnips were made to look like roses, and other vegetables were often shaped into flowers. A curl of carrot is about all that is left of that style.

Garnishes not only decorate or adorn, but can provide essential proteins, vitamins, and minerals. A sprinkling of nuts, sunflower seeds, grated cheese, wheat germ, or bean sprouts is added "health insurance," it provides flavor and texture in your salad.

Eye appeal, which also stimulates the taste buds, is usually brought about by some contrasting colors and textures. If your salad needs the sharp color-zing of red, use julienne beets, sliced or minced pimiento, chopped or diced sweet red pepper, or even a shaving of red cabbage. Shades of green can be provided by adding minced chives, parsley, watercress, tiny spinach leaves, and olives on a light colored leaf. Other contrasting colors may be achieved by using grated or diced cheese, hard-cooked eggs, grated carrots, capers, and black olives.

There are many garnishes to provide texture contrast. Crisp ones, such as bread croutons, bacon bits, sliced water chestnuts, seeds of cardamom, caraway, or sunflower, and chopped or whole nuts, are especially appropriate on soft greens. For firm salads use soft garnishes such as slivers of tomato flesh, sliced mushrooms, and grated egg or cheese.

Some garnishes are more flavorful than others, those belonging to the onion family being among the most pungent. Don't overwhelm a delicate salad with lots of scallions, caraway seeds, and radishes. They are so strong in flavor they could easily overpower more subtle flavors. As you can see, there are quantities of garnishes to choose from in order to get just the right touch to pep up your salad.

Calorie Chart

Fruits and Vegetables

APRICOT 1 raw	18
½ cup, canned, water-packed	47
APPLE 1 medium, peeled	85
ARTICHOKE 1 medium	55
ASPARAGUS 6 thick spears, fresh	30
6 thick spears, canned	19
AVOCADO 1	302
cup, cubed	251
BANANA 1 medium	101
BAMBOO SHOOTS ½ cup	20
BEANS, GREEN ½ cup	15
BEANS, LIMA ½ cup, fresh	95
BEAN SPROUTS, MUNG 1 cup	37
BEAN SPROUTS, SOY 1 cup	48
BEAN SPROUTS, ALFALFA 1 cup	23
BEETS ½ cup, diced, fresh	27
½ cup, diced, canned	30
BLUEBERRIES ½ cup, raw	45
BROCCOLI ½ cup	20
½ cup, frozen	25
BULGUR WHEAT ½ cup	300
CABBAGE 1 cup, shredded	20
CABBAGE, RED 1 cup	28
CABBAGE, CHINESE 1 cup	11
CANTALOUPE ¼ medium melon	20
CARROTS ½ cup, diced, fresh	22
CAULIFLOWER 1 cup, flowerettes	27
CELERY 1 stalk	7
1 cup, diced	20
CHERRIES ½ cup	45
½ cup, canned, water-packed	60

CALORIES

CORN	½ cup, fresh	70
	½ cup, canned	87
CRESS	1 cup, chopped	78
CUCUMBER	1 cup, sliced	16
EGGPLANT	1 cup, diced	38
ENDIVE, BELGIAN	½ pound (two servings)	40
ESCAROLE	1 cup	10
FRUIT COCKTAIL	½ cup, water-packed	45
GRAPEFRUIT	½ medium	40
GRAPES, SEEDLESS	½ cup	50
HONEYDEW MELON	¼ medium	56
KALE	1 cup, cubed	43
KOHLRABI	1 cup, diced	41
LEEKS	½ cup, cut up (5 pieces)	50
LEMON JUICE	1 tablespoon	4
LETTUCE, BOSTON	½ head	12
LETTUCE, BIBB	1 head	12
LETTUCE, ICEBERG	1 cup, chopped	10
LETTUCE, LOOSE LEAF	1 cup, chopped	10
LETTUCE, ROMAINE	1 cup, chopped	10
MUSHROOMS	½ cup, sliced	10
	½ cup, canned	15
OLIVES, GREEN	4 medium	20
OLIVES, BLACK	4 large	30
ONIONS, GREEN (SCALLIONS)	2 tablespoons, chopped	15
ONIONS, CHIVES	2 teaspoons, chopped	6
ORANGES	1 whole, medium	50
	½ cup, segments	45
PAPAYA	1 cup, diced	55
PARSLEY	2 tablespoons, chopped	4
PEACH	1 large, fresh	38
	½ cup, sliced	32
	½ cup, canned, water-packed	37
PEAR	1 medium, fresh	100
	½ cup, canned, water-packed	40
PEAS	½ cup, fresh	61
	½ cup, frozen	54
PEPPERS, GREEN OR RED	1 large	22
PINEAPPLE	½ cup, raw diced	40
	1 large slice, canned, water-packed	48
PLUMS	1 large prune-type	21

CALORIES

POTATO 1 medium	86
PRUNES 5 medium	82
RADISHES 6 medium	5
RAISINS 1 tablespoon	26
RASPBERRIES ½ cup	35
SHALLOTS 1 tablespoon, minced	7
SPINACH 1 cup, chopped	14
STRAWBERRIES 1 cup	55
TOMATO 1 medium	25
½ cup, diced	39
TURNIP 1 cup, sliced, raw	39
WATERMELON 1 cup, diced	42
ZUCCHINI 1 cup, diced or sliced	22

Fish

*(all canned fish is water-packed
except where specified)*

ANCHOVIES 2 ounces	100
ANCHOVY PASTE 1 teaspoon	14
CRAB MEAT 1 cup, flaked, fresh	116
1 cup, canned	136
LOBSTER MEAT 1 cup, fresh	138
4 ounces, canned	95
SALMON 4 ounces, canned	120
SARDINES 4 ounces	160
4 ounces in oil	350
SHRIMP 4 ounces, fresh	132
1 cup, canned	148
TUNA 1 7-ounce can	251
WHITEFISH, COD, BASS,	
HALIBUT, OR SIMILAR FISH 2 ounces	100

Cheese

BLUE, ROQUEFORT 1 ounce	105
CHEDDAR 1 ounce, grated	113
COTTAGE 1 cup	125
1 cup, creamed, small curd	223
CREAM 1 tablespoon	52
PARMESAN 1 tablespoon, grated	21

Eggs

	CALORIES
EGG 1	75
YOLK 1	52
WHITE 1	15

Salad Dressings

OLIVE OIL 1 tablespoon	120
VEGETABLE OILS 1 tablespoon	120
VINEGAR 1 tablespoon	2
BLUE CHEESE, ROQUEFORT 1 tablespoon	76
1 tablespoon, low-calorie	12
BUTTERMILK 1 tablespoon	15
COOKED 1 tablespoon	25
FRENCH 1 tablespoon	88
FRENCH, COMMERCIAL 1 tablespoon	66
FRENCH-TYPE, COMMERCIAL, LOW-CALORIE 1 tablespoon	15
ITALIAN 1 tablespoon	83
1 tablespoon, low-calorie	8
MAYONNAISE 1 tablespoon	101
MAYONNAISE-TYPE, COMMERCIAL 1 tablespoon	65
MAYONNAISE, LOW-CALORIE 1 tablespoon	22
RUSSIAN 1 tablespoon	74
THOUSAND ISLAND 1 tablespoon	80

ONE

The Side Salad

an accompaniment

The perfect way for health-conscious chefs to enliven a main dish is by serving a delicious side salad. Easily prepared ahead of time or at the last minute, salads provide important nutrients without adding a lot of calories. A side salad no longer means hearts of lettuce smothered with commercial dressing. The recipes in this chapter offer a variety of vegetables from Belgian endives to crunchy raw turnips.

A good rule for choosing a side salad is let your entrée be your guide. A crisp vegetable salad with lemon french dressing peps up a creamed main course, while cold roasted meats are complemented by a creamy potato salad.

Some salads and main courses seem naturally to belong together: apple-beet salad with pork; cole slaw with ham or baked beans; cucumbers with fish. You can also try unusual but tasty combinations like soy ginger spinach with beef, cooked zucchini salad with lasagne, or endive and beet salad with veal. Choose side salads that add variety, contrast, and just the right accent to your meal!

Apple-Beet Salad

   2 cups peeled and diced tart apples (2 medium)
   2 cups diced pickled beets
  ⅓ cup pickle relish
  ¼ cup minced onion
  ¼ cup mayonnaise*
   1 tablespoon sugar
   2 tablespoons cider vinegar
  ¼ teaspoon salt
  ⅛ teaspoon freshly ground pepper
    Lettuce leaves
   1 hard-cooked egg

Place apples and beets in a bowl. Gently mix with relish, onion, mayonnaise, sugar, cider vinegar, salt, and pepper. Spoon into lettuce-lined serving dish and garnish with chopped egg. Makes 4 servings.

Blueberry-Radish Salad

    1 teaspoon grated orange rind
     Juice of 1 orange
   ⅓ cup salad oil
    2 tablespoons minced parsley
     Salt
     Freshly ground white pepper
    6 cups torn escarole (or mixed greens if
        preferred)
1 ½ cups coarsely shredded radishes
    1 cup fresh blueberries

Combine orange rind, orange juice, oil, and parsley and mix well. Season with salt and white pepper. Put escarole

in bowl. Top with radishes, then sprinkle with blueberries. Just before serving, add dressing and toss. Makes
6 servings.

Broccoli and Chickpeas Vinaigrette

    1 bunch broccoli
      Boiling salted water
    1 can (20 ounces) chickpeas or white kidney
        beans, drained
    ¼ cup minced red pepper or pimientos
    ⅓ cup oil
    3 tablespoons vinegar
      Salt
      Freshly ground pepper

Cut broccoli in flowerettes with about one-inch stalk on
each (reserve remaining stalks for soups, stews, or casseroles). Steam flowerettes in small amount of boiling
salted water 5 to 7 minutes or until tender; drain. In bowl
combine broccoli, chickpeas, red pepper, oil, and vinegar. Sprinkle with salt and pepper to taste. Serve warm
or chilled. Makes 4 to 6 servings.

Cucumbers in Sour Cream

    3 medium cucumbers, peeled and sliced thin
    3 teaspoons salt
    ½ teaspoon pepper
    1 teaspoon sugar
    2 teaspoons minced parsley
    1 teaspoon minced onion
    1 cup dairy sour cream

Sprinkle the sliced cucumbers with salt and let them stand for several hours. Rinse under cold water and drain. Place them in a bowl. Combine pepper, sugar, parsley, onion, and sour cream and stir into the cucumbers. Serve chilled. Makes 6 servings.

Marinated Green-Bean and Carrot Salad

    ½ cup water
    1 package (9 ounces) frozen whole green beans
    1 cup sliced carrots, about ¼-inch thick
    ½ cup sliced celery
    3 tablespoons lemon juice
    2 tablespoons oil
    1 tablespoon minced onion
    ½ teaspoon salt
      Dash of pepper
    ¼ teaspoon oregano

Bring water to boil; add beans and carrots and simmer 4 to 5 minutes or until tender but still crisp; drain. Combine the beans and carrots with the celery. Mix in the lemon juice, oil, onion, and seasonings. Cover and chill at least 4 hours or overnight, stirring occasionally. Makes 4 servings.

Belgian Endive and Orange Salad

    4 Belgian endives
    3 large oranges
    2 tablespoons fresh orange juice
    2 tablespoons Lemon French Dressing*

Cut the ends from the endives. Wash, dry, and slice them crosswise into ½-inch pieces. Peel the oranges with a sharp knife, removing all white pith, and section the fruit. In a bowl combine oranges and endive. And the orange juice to the dressing, pour over the salad, and toss gently. Makes 6 servings.

Endive and Beet Salad

    4 heads Belgian endive
    1 can (1 pound) whole baby beets, drained
    ½ cup French Dressing*

Cut the ends from the endives and slice in half lengthwise. Wash and dry. Cut them crosswise into bite-size pieces and place in a low salad bowl or on 6 individual plates. Arrange the beets on the endive and pour the dressing over the salad. Makes 6 servings.

Escarole, Spinach, and Bacon Vinaigrette

    1 bunch (about 1½ pounds) escarole
   ¾ to 1 pound fresh spinach
      Salt to taste
    2 slices bacon
    1 medium onion, quartered and sliced
    2 tablespoons cider vinegar

Rinse escarole and spinach in cold water, remove tough stems, tear leaves in small pieces, and drain. Steam with only the water clinging to the leaves in large covered kettle over medium heat 8 to 10 minutes, or until tender. Season with a little salt. Fry bacon until crisp; drain and crumble. Sauté onion in bacon drippings until golden brown and tender; blend in vinegar, pour over escarole and spinach, and toss to coat. Sprinkle with bacon. Makes 4 to 6 servings.

Marinated Mushroom-Spinach Salad

½ cup oil
¼ cup white wine vinegar
2 tablespoons minced onion
½ teaspoon basil
1 teaspoon salt
¼ teaspoon freshly ground pepper
½ pound mushrooms, sliced thin
1 pound young spinach, torn into bite-size pieces

Combine oil, vinegar, onion, basil, salt, and pepper in a bowl. Add mushrooms and marinate at room temperature for 2 hours, or refrigerate overnight, stirring occasionally. Place spinach in a salad bowl; add mushroom-oil mixture and toss well. Makes 6 servings.

Special Spinach Salad

1 pound raw young spinach, washed and torn
    into bite-size pieces
4 scallions, chopped, or 1 sweet onion cut
    in rings
½ cup French Dressing*
1 clove garlic, crushed
2 tablespoons sour cream
¼ teaspoon rosemary
6 slices bacon, cooked and crumbled

Arrange spinach in a salad bowl with the scallions or onion rings. Whip the dressing, garlic, sour cream, and rosemary and pour over the salad. Toss well and sprinkle with the crumbled bacon. Makes 6 servings.

Soy-Ginger Spinach Salad

    1 package (10 ounces) fresh spinach
    1 can (8 ounces) water chestnuts, drained and
        sliced thin
    3 tablespoons water
    2 tablespoons cider vinegar
    2 tablespoons soy sauce
    4 teaspoons oil
    ½ teaspoon sugar
    ⅛ teaspoon ground ginger
    1 small clove garlic, crushed
    1 tablespoon sesame seed, toasted

Rinse spinach well. Tear leaves from stems (discard stems). Drain leaves and dry on paper towels. Place spinach and water chestnuts in salad bowl. In a jar with tight-fitting lid shake water, vinegar, soy sauce, oil, sugar, ginger, and garlic. Pour over salad, sprinkle with sesame seed, and toss lightly. Makes 6 servings.

Cold Spinach-Yogurt Puree

    1 pound spinach, washed thoroughly
    1 clove garlic, crushed
    ½ teaspoon salt
    ¼ teaspoon freshly ground pepper
    2 tablespoons lemon juice

> 1 tablespoon fresh minced or 1 teaspoon
>   crushed dry mint leaves
> 1 tablespoon minced onion
> 2 cups plain yogurt

Remove heavy stems from the spinach and cook it with only the water that clings to the leaves until it is limp, 2 or 3 minutes. Drain and mix in a blender or food processor with the garlic, salt, pepper, lemon juice, mint, and onion. Put mixture into a bowl and stir in the yogurt. Adjust seasoning and chill. Makes 4 servings.

Cherry-Tomato and Watercress Salad

> 1 bunch watercress
> 3 cups cherry tomatoes, cut into halves
> 3 tablespoons cider vinegar
> ⅓ cup oil
> 1 teaspoon salt
> ¼ teaspoon freshly ground pepper
> 1 teaspoon sugar
> 1½ cups cheese or garlic-flavored croutons

Remove heavy stems from watercress and chop the leaves very fine. Place the tomatoes, vinegar, oil, salt, pepper, and sugar in a bowl. Add watercress and toss gently. Arrange salad on individual plates and sprinkle with croutons. Makes 6 servings.

Tomatoes with Fines Herbes

> 3 large tomatoes, peeled and sliced
> 3 tablespoons oil
> 2 tablespoons vinegar

½ teaspoon salt
¼ teaspoon sugar
¼ teaspoon freshly ground pepper
1 teaspoon fresh or ¼ teaspoon dried tarragon
   or basil
1 tablespoon minced chives
1 tablespoon minced parsley

Arrange the tomatoes in overlapping slices on a serving dish. Mix together the oil, vinegar, salt, sugar, pepper, and herbs. Pour over the tomatoes and let stand at room temperature for several hours. Chill slightly just before serving if you wish. Makes 4 to 6 servings.

VARIATIONS

I. Tomatoes with Blue Cheese: Follow recipe for Tomatoes with Fines Herbes* but eliminate tarragon, basil, and chives. Just before serving, sprinkle tomatoes with ¼ pound crumbled blue cheese.

II. Tomatoes with Red Onion: Follow recipe for Tomatoes with Fines Herbes.* Arrange a sliced red onion, separated into rings, over tomatoes before adding the dressing.

Tomato-Zucchini-Yogurt Salad

2 zucchini, unpeeled and sliced thin
1 green pepper, coarsely chopped
½ sweet onion, coarsely chopped
1 container (8 ounces) plain yogurt
½ teaspoon dillweed
½ teaspoon salt
   Freshly ground pepper to taste
2 tomatoes, cut in wedges

Combine zucchini, green pepper, and onion with the yogurt, dillweed, salt, and pepper. Add tomatoes and toss lightly. Serve in crisp lettuce cups. Makes 4 to 6 servings.

Crunchy Turnip Salad

3 cups peeled, thinly sliced white turnips
2 apples, unpeeled and sliced thin
3 scallions, chopped fine
3 tablespoons soy sauce
1 tablespoon sugar
½ cup French Dressing*
Lettuce

Combine the turnips, apples, and scallions in a bowl. Add soy and sugar to the french dressing and shake well. Pour over the salad, toss and chill. Serve on Boston or Bibb lettuce. Makes 6 servings.

Cooked Zucchini Salad

1 pound zucchini, unpeeled
2 tablespoons olive oil
½ cup French Dressing*
1 clove garlic, crushed
1 tablespoon minced parsley

Slice the zucchini thin and sauté in olive oil until crisp-tender. Cool slightly and mix with the dressing and garlic. Spoon into a serving bowl, sprinkle with parsley, and chill. Makes 4 servings.

TWO

The Appetizer Salad
before the meal begins

The custom of serving salads as a first course originated in California and it is no wonder that the idea soon swept the country. Crudités—raw vegetables—popular for their fresh flavor, crunchiness, and low calorie count, make ideal hors d'oeuvres at a cocktail party. Vary conventional vegetables with some unusual choices: thin slices of kohlrabi, tiny green beans, strips of white turnip, thin green asparagus, and crunchy fennel slices.

Salads are perfect to whet the appetite without being too filling. For a sit-down dinner serve three-dimensional salads such as ripe stuffed tomatoes or artichokes vinaigrette. Other delicious beginnings might include mushrooms with fennel, clam aspic, a lobster and grapefruit combination, tossed tender greens, or a zesty antipasto platter.

Antipasto

  1 head romaine lettuce
  1 package (10 ounces) frozen artichoke hearts,
        cooked as directed on package
¼ cup Vinaigrette Dressing*
¼ pound salami cut in strips
¼ pound provolone, cubed
¼ pound ham, cut in strips
  1 jar (7½ ounces) roasted red peppers, drained

    1 can (2 ounces) anchovies, drained
    2 tablespoons capers
      Black olives
      Stuffed olives
    3 hard-cooked eggs, cut in half
    2 tomatoes, peeled and cut in wedges
 1 ½ cups Italian Dressing*

Rinse romaine and tear into pieces; crisp in refrigerator. Marinate cooked artichoke hearts in ¼ cup vinaigrette dressing. On a large platter, make a bed of romaine leaves. Arrange artichoke hearts in center and place remaining ingredients around the edge, grouping salami and provolone; ham; red peppers, anchovies, and capers; black and stuffed olives; egg halves and tomato wedges. Serve with the italian dressing. Makes 6 servings.

Artichokes Vinaigrette

    6 globe artichokes
      Boiling salted water
    2 tablespoons vinegar or one lemon, sliced
 1 ½ cups Vinaigrette* or French Dressing*

Slice the stalk of the artichokes straight across so the vegetable will stand up. Pull off the lower leaves if they are dry or discolored. Trim the tops of the leaves with scissors and cut 1 inch off the very top leaves with a sharp knife. Boil the artichokes, stem side down, in deep salted water with vinegar or lemon slices. To test for doneness pull off a leaf; if it comes out easily, the artichokes are ready. It will take from 30 to 40 minutes. Drain upside down and chill. Serve with 4 tablespoons of dressing in a small dish on the side or in the well of artichoke plates. Makes 6 servings.

VARIATION

Artichokes Mayonnaise: Proceed as for Artichokes Vinaigrette* substituting mayonnaise for the Vinaigrette* or French Dressing.* Makes 6 servings.

Stuffed Artichokes

6 artichokes
  Boiling salted water
2 tablespoons vinegar or one lemon, sliced
2 cups cooked diced chicken or shrimp
1 cup chopped celery
2 tablespoons minced parsley
1 tablespoon lemon juice
½ cup plus 2 tablespoons Mayonnaise*

Trim, cook, drain, and cool artichokes according to directions for Artichokes Vinaigrette.* Spread the leaves of the artichoke apart, pull out center yellow leaves, and scrape out the spiny choke with a spoon. Combine chicken or shrimp with celery, parsley, lemon juice, and ½ cup mayonnaise; mix well. Fill the center of each artichoke with the mixture and press the leaves back together. Top each with a dollop of the remaining mayonnaise. Additional mayonnaise may by served as a dip for the leaves. Makes 6 servings.

Asparagus Salad

>   2 pounds asparagus, scraped and cut into
>   1-inch pieces
>   ¼ cup oil
>   2 tablespoons vinegar
>   2 tablespoons soy sauce
>   1 teaspoon sugar
>   Salad greens (optional)

Cook the asparagus until crisp-tender, not more than 5
minutes. Drain and chill. Combine the oil, vinegar, soy
sauce, and sugar and mix thoroughly. Pour over the
asparagus and chill for at least an hour. Serve in 6
individual glass bowls or on lettuce-lined salad plates.
Makes 6 servings.

Avocado-Grapefruit Mold

>   1 package (3 ounces) lemon gelatin
>   1 cup boiling water
>   1 to 2 grapefruits, pink preferred
>   1 medium avocado, peeled and sliced
>   ½ cup Lemon French* or Fruit French
>   Dressing*

Dissolve gelatin in boiling water. Peel a large grapefruit, then section over bowl or large measure to catch
juice. Add enough water to juice to make 1 cup and stir
into dissolved gelatin. Pour about 1 inch of gelatin mixture into a wet 1-quart mold (melon-shaped, if available).
Refrigerate until thickened and very syrupy. Arrange
about half the grapefruit sections and avocado slices in
alternate rows in bottom of mold. Refrigerate until almost

set. Pour in the rest of the gelatin and arrange remaining grapefruit and avocado where necessary. Chill until firm. Unmold on serving platter and garnish with additional grapefruit sections, if desired. Serve with salad dressing. Makes 4 to 6 servings.

Avocado with Frozen Tomato Mayonnaise

    4 medium avocados, chilled
    2 tablespoons lemon juice
      Watercress
      Frozen Tomato Mayonnaise*

Peel the avocados with a sharp knife. Cut in half, remove pits, and sprinkle on all sides with lemon juice. Place on watercress-lined glass plates and fill the centers with frozen tomato mayonnaise. Makes 8 servings.

Beet and Egg Salad

    2 cups canned julienne beets, drained, or
         fresh-cooked julienne beets
    4 hard-cooked eggs, sliced
    1 cup chopped watercress leaves
    1 tablespoon grated onion
    ½ teaspoon thyme
    ½ cup French Dressing*

Place the beets and eggs in a salad bowl with the watercress. Add the onion and thyme to the french dressing. Pour over the salad and toss very gently. Serve at once. Makes 4 servings.

Borsch Aspic

> 1 cup canned julienne beets, drained
> 1 can (10½ ounces) beef consommé
> 1 package (3 ounces) lemon gelatin
> 2 tablespoons vinegar
> 1 tablespoon grated onion
> 1 teaspoon salt
> 1 cup finely shredded cabbage
>   Shredded lettuce
>   Horseradish Dressing*

Add enough liquid from the beets and water to consommé to make 2 cups. Heat to boiling. Pour over gelatin and stir until dissolved. Stir in vinegar, onion, and salt. Chill until syrupy. Fold in beets and cabbage. Turn into a wet 8-inch-square pan and chill until firm. Unmold and cut in squares; serve on shredded lettuce with dressing. Makes 4 servings.

Celeriac Salad

> 1 large or 2 small celeriac, peeled
> 2 tablespoons lemon juice
> 1 teaspoon prepared mustard
> ½ cup Mayonnaise*
>   Salt
>   Freshly ground pepper

Cut the celeriac into julienne strips and boil for 2 minutes. Drain at once, sprinkle with lemon juice, and chill. Add the mustard to the mayonnaise and mix. Pour over the celeriac and toss thoroughly. Season to taste with salt and pepper and chill. Makes 4 servings.

Clam Aspic

  2 envelopes unflavored gelatin
  1 cup clam juice
  1 can (8 ounces) minced clams, undrained
  1 teaspoon lemon juice
  1 cup vegetable juice cocktail
  1 pint cottage cheese
  2 tablespoons dairy sour cream
  1 tablespoon minced parsley
    Mayonnaise*

Soften the gelatin in ½ cup clam juice. Heat the remaining clam juice, clams and their liquid, lemon juice, and vegetable juice cocktail. Add the softened gelatin; heat and stir until gelatin is dissolved. Pour into a wet one-quart ring mold. Chill until set. Unmold on a cool serving plate. Combine cottage cheese with sour cream and spoon into center of mold. Sprinkle with parsley and serve with mayonnaise. Makes 6 servings.

Crab Mousse

  2 envelopes unflavored gelatin
  ¼ cup cold water
  ½ cup boiling fish broth, clam juice, or water
1 ½ cups flaked crab meat
  ½ cup minced celery
  ¼ cup minced carrots
  2 tablespoons minced parsley
  1 tablespoon lemon juice
  ½ cup Mayonnaise*
  ⅓ cup heavy cream, whipped
    Salt
    Freshly ground white pepper
    Shredded lettuce

Soften the gelatin in ¼ cup cold water; dissolve in boiling liquid. Combine the crab meat, celery, carrots, parsley, and lemon juice with the mayonnaise, and blend well. Stir in the gelatin mixture. Fold in whipped cream and season to taste with salt and pepper. Spoon into a wet one-quart loaf pan or mold and chill until firm. Unmold on shredded lettuce. Makes 6 servings.

Egg-Spinach-Shrimp Salad

    10 hard-cooked eggs, halved
     1 package (10 ounces) frozen chopped
            spinach, cooked, well drained, and cooled
    ½ cup Mayonnaise*
    ½ cup dairy sour cream
     1 cup cooked shrimp, finely chopped
     1 tablespoon lemon juice
       Salt
       White pepper
       Shredded lettuce
     5 tablespoons red or black caviar
       Dill sprigs

Carefully separate egg yolks from whites and chop yolks fine. Remove ⅓ cup and set aside. Reserve 10 egg-white halves and chop remainder. In mixing bowl, combine chopped egg yolks and whites with spinach, mayonnaise, sour cream, shrimp, and lemon juice. Mix well and season to taste with salt and pepper. Line a serving platter with lettuce. Reserve ⅓ cup shrimp mixture and pour remainder in center. Arrange reserved egg-white halves around edge. Fill halves alternately with reserved shrimp mixture and with caviar. Garnish center salad with reserved chopped egg yolk and dill sprigs. Chill. Makes 5 servings as luncheon dish or 10 as appetizer.

Feta Cheese and Eggplant Salad

    1 large eggplant
    1 small onion, chopped
    ¼ cup olive oil
    2 tablespoons lemon juice
      Salt
      Freshly ground pepper
      Chopped parsley
      Sliced tomatoes
      Black olives
      Green-pepper strips
      Sweet onion slices
      Cubes of Greek feta cheese

Put whole eggplant in shallow baking dish and bake in preheated 400°F oven 45 minutes, or until soft. Remove skin and dice eggplant. Add onion, oil, lemon juice, and salt and pepper to taste; chill. Place on a large platter and sprinkle with parsley. Surround with sliced tomatoes, olives, green-pepper strips, onion slices, and feta cheese. Makes 6 to 8 servings.

Gazpacho Salad Mold

    1 envelope unflavored gelatin
    1⅔ cups tomato juice
    2 tablespoons wine vinegar
    1 large tomato, peeled, seeded, and chopped
    1 cucumber, peeled, seeded, and chopped
    1 canned green chili, well drained, seeded,
        and chopped
    ¼ cup sliced green onions
    1 clove garlic, minced

¾ teaspoon salt
⅛ teaspoon freshly ground pepper
Pinch of sugar
Crisp salad greens

Soften gelatin in ¼ cup tomato juice. Heat remaining juice. Add softened gelatin and stir until thoroughly dissolved. Add vinegar, tomato, cucumber, chili, onions, garlic, salt, pepper, and sugar and pour into a wet one-quart mold. Chill overnight, or until set. Unmold on a platter lined with greens. Makes 4 to 6 servings.

Molded Guacamole Salad

1 envelope unflavored gelatin
1 cup cold water
3 tablespoons lemon juice
1 clove garlic, crushed
2 teaspoons grated onion
1 teaspoon salt
Dash of hot pepper sauce
1½ cups mashed avocado
⅓ cup Mayonnaise*
Crisp greens
Mayonnaise* (optional)

Sprinkle gelatin over cold water in small saucepan. Cook and stir over low heat until gelatin dissolves, about 3 minutes. Add lemon juice, garlic, onion, salt, pepper sauce, avocado, and mayonnaise; stir until well blended. Turn into a wet one-quart mold and chill until firm. Unmold on greens. Serve with additional mayonnaise and crips corn chips, if you wish. Makes 6 servings.

Mushroom-Fennel Salad

1 pound fresh mushrooms
2 fennel hearts
½ cup Mayonnaise*
1 tablespoon prepared mustard
½ teaspoon salt
½ teaspoon oregano
  Lettuce

Wipe mushrooms and slice them thin. Trim the base of the fennel and chop into ¼-inch pieces. Combine mayonnaise, mustard, salt, and oregano and mix thoroughly with the mushrooms and fennel. Serve on a bed of lettuce. Makes 6 servings.

Lobster Salad

1¼ pounds cooked lobster meat
1 cup diced celery
1 tablespoon lemon juice
1 tablespoon white wine
¼ cup heavy cream, whipped
½ cup Mayonnaise*
  Salad greens
12 peeled grapefruit sections

Cut the lobster into small bite-size pieces and combine with the celery. Moisten with lemon juice and wine and chill for several hours. Fold the whipped cream into the mayonnaise. Place the lobster on a platter lined with crisp mixed greens. Garnish with sections of grapefruit. Spoon dressing over the lobster and toss. Makes 4 to 6 servings.

Oyster Salad

> 1 quart of oysters with juice
> Water
> ½ cup Mayonnaise*
> 1 teaspoon tarragon
> 1 teaspoon prepared horseradish
> 1 teaspoon lemon juice
> 1 teaspoon grated onion
> Few drops hot pepper sauce
> Shredded lettuce
> Minced parsley

Drain the oysters. Combine the juice with 1 cup water and bring the liquid to a boil. Poach the oysters for 1 to 2 minutes until the edges begin to curl. Drain, cover with plastic wrap, and chill. Blend the mayonnaise with tarragon, horseradish, lemon juice, onion, and hot pepper sauce. Arrange the oysters on a lettuce-lined serving plate. Spoon the dressing over the salad and garnish with parsley. Makes 6 servings.

Melons Filled with Shrimp and Grapes

> 4 small cantaloupes, chilled, halved, and seeded
> 1½ pounds cooked small shrimp
> 1 pound small seedless grapes
> 1 cup Italian Dressing*
> 8 sprigs mint

Scoop all meat out of 8 melon halves. Drain and reserve shells. Dice melon meat and combine with shrimp, grapes, and dressing. Cover and marinate in the refrigerator for at least one hour. Just before serving spoon shrimp mixture into drained melon halves and garnish with sprigs of mint. Makes 8 servings.

Tomatoes Stuffed With Egg Salad

 4 tomatoes
 4 hard-cooked eggs, chopped
 2 tablespoons minced onion or scallions
 1 tablespoon minced parsley
 ½ cup Mayonnaise*
 1 teaspoon Worcestershire sauce
 ½ teaspoon basil
 ½ teaspoon salt
   Freshly ground pepper
   Watercress sprigs

Cut the tops off the tomatoes. Scoop out the flesh, drain, and chop it. Mix 1 cup of tomato flesh with the eggs, onion, parsley, mayonnaise, Worcestershire sauce, and basil. Season with salt and pepper. Fill the tomatoes and replace the tops if you wish. Garnish with sprigs of watercress. Makes 4 servings.

VARIATION

Tomatoes Stuffed with Shrimp Salad: Substitute ½ cup cooked, cut-up shrimp for the eggs in Tomatoes Stuffed with Egg Salad* and add 1 teaspoon lemon juice to the Mayonnaise.*

Vegetables in Aspic

  1 envelope unflavored gelatin
  ¼ cup cold water
  1 cup chicken broth
  ¼ cup tomato juice
12 cooked asparagus tips
  1 cup cooked peas
  1 cup cooked diced carrots
    Salad greens
    Mayonnaise*

Soften the gelatin in cold water. Add to the broth, place over boiling water, and stir until dissolved. Add tomato juice and mix. Pour ¼ inch of aspic into the bottom of a one-quart mold and chill until set. Place the asparagus tips spoke-fashion with the tips pointing out on the aspic and refrigerate. Chill remaining aspic until syrupy and combine with peas and carrots. Pour this mixture over the asparagus in the mold; chill until set. Unmold onto salad greens and serve with mayonnaise. Makes 4 to 6 servings.

THREE

The International Salad

everyone eats salad

Today it's not necessary to cross an ocean or even to go to a foreign restaurant to sample international fare. Fortunately, most food specialty shops and many supermarkets now offer all the necessary ingredients—from fish roe for a Greek taramasalata to bulgur for an Iranian tabbouleh—to produce exotic salads in your own home.

Delight your friends with a Mexican meal beginning with a zesty guacamole, or plan a Hawaiian buffet featuring lomi lomi, a smoked salmon salad, and Hawaiian bean-sprout salad. The flavors of other countries are no farther than your own kitchen.

Chinese-Cabbage Salad

        2 small cucumbers, peeled and sliced thin
      ⅓ cup finely chopped scallions
        4 cups thinly sliced Chinese cabbage
      ½ cup thinly sliced radishes
        1 cup dairy sour cream
    1½ tablespoons soy sauce
        2 tablespoons rice vinegar

In salad bowl, combine and toss cucumbers, scallions, cabbage, and radishes. Cover and chill. Mix the sour cream with soy sauce and vinegar. Pour over salad and toss. Makes 6 servings.

Oriental Chicken-Sesame Salad

    2 cups cooked chicken, cut in julienne strips
    2 tablespoons soy sause
    6 tablespoons salad oil
    1 clove garlic, crushed
    1 teaspoon grated lemon rind
    3 cups spinach leaves, cut in strips
    3 cups thinly sliced Chinese cabbage
    2 tablespoons lemon juice
    ½ teaspoon salt
    2 tablespoons toasted sesame seed

Marinate chicken several hours in 1 tablespoon soy sauce,
2 tablespoons oil, the garlic, and ½ teaspoon lemon rind.
Just before serving, toss spinach and cabbage with remaining oil, lemon rind, lemon juice, and salt. Add
chicken and sesame seed and mix thoroughly. Makes 8
servings.

Bouillabaisse Salad

    ½ pound halibut, poached and chilled
    ½ pound salmon, poached and chilled
    ½ pound cooked shrimp
    ½ pound cooked crab or lobster meat
    16 raw shelled clams or oysters (optional)
    1½ cups Lemon French Dressing*
       Watercress or parsley
    8 lemon wedges

Divide the chilled halibut, salmon, shrimp, and shellfish
into 8 portions. Place the fish, alternating color and
textures, in 8 individual open soup plates. Pour three

tablespoons dressing over each serving and garnish with watercress or parsley and lemon wedges. Makes 8 servings.

Salade Parisienne

    1 cup cooked cut green beans
    1 cup cooked green peas
    1 cup cooked cauliflowerettes
    1 cup coarsely shredded carrots
    ½ pound sliced mushrooms
    ¼ pound cooked diced chicken livers
    ½ pound small cooked shrimp
    ½ cup French Dressing*
    2 tablespoons heavy cream
      Salt
      Freshly ground pepper

Place beans, peas, cauliflowerettes, carrots, mushrooms, chicken livers, and shrimp in a bowl; mix well, cover, and chill. Combine the dressing with the cream, pour over the salad, and toss. Season to taste with salt and pepper. Makes 8 servings.

German Wilted Lettuce

    2 heads garden lettuce, or any soft lettuce
    4 slices bacon
    3 teaspoons sugar
    ⅓ cup vinegar

Wash the lettuce, dry it, and break into bite-size pieces. Sauté the bacon until crisp, remove, and dry on paper towel. Crumble it over the lettuce in a salad bowl. Add the sugar and vinegar to the bacon drippings, bring to a boil, and pour over the lettuce. Toss and serve at once. Makes 6 servings.

Greek Supper Salad

          5 medium potatoes
          2 tablespoons minced parsley
          2 tablespoons chopped scallion
          2 tablespoons salad oil
          1 tablespoon cider vinegar
          1 teaspoon salt
         ¼ teaspoon freshly ground pepper
         ⅓ cup Mayonnaise*
         ½ bunch watercress, chopped
          4 cups shredded salad greens (escarole,
               chicory, and/or lettuce)
          2 large tomatoes, peeled and cut in wedges
          1 avocado, peeled, halved, and sliced
          1 cucumber, peeled and cut in spears
          1 large green pepper, seeded and sliced in rings
          1 red onion, thinly sliced and separated into rings
         ½ cup Greek-style black olives
         ¼ pound feta cheese, diced
          1 bunch radishes, washed and trimmed
       1½ cups French Dressing*

Cook, peel, and dice potatoes. While still warm mix them with parsley, scallions, oil, vinegar, salt, and pepper; add mayonnaise and toss. Cover and chill until ready to serve. Place watercress and greens on a large platter. Mound potatoes in center and arrange tomato wedges, avocado, cucumber, green pepper, onion, black olives, and cheese on greens around edge of platter. Garnish with radishes. Serve with dressing. Makes 8 servings.

Taramasalata (Greek Fish Roe Salad)

8 ounces tarama (fish roe)
4 tablespoons lemon juice
3 slices white bread, crusts off
1 cup olive oil

Combine the tarama with the lemon juice in a blender or food processor. Wet the bread and squeeze dry. Add the bread and blend well with the tarama. Add the oil slowly while blending until mixture is thick and light colored. Cover and chill. If used as a canapé dip, serve with thin toast or pita bread. If presented as a first course, garnish with tomato wedges, cucumber slices, and Greek olives. Makes 6 servings.

Hawaiian Bean-Sprout Salad

2 pounds fresh bean sprouts
1 green or red pepper, diced
3 scallions, chopped
2 tablespoons toasted sesame seeds
2 tablespoons vinegar
2 tablespoons peanut or sesame oil
2 tablespoons soy sauce
2 tablespoons sugar

Blanch sprouts by placing them in a colander and pouring boiling water over them. Drain and combine with the pepper and scallions in a bowl. Mix sesame seeds, vinegar, oil, soy sauce, and sugar; pour over the salad and toss. Serve warm or chilled. Makes 8 servings.

Lomi Lomi (Hawaiian Salmon Salad)

1 pound smoked or salted salmon, thinly sliced
4 tomatoes, peeled and diced
4 scallions, chopped
1 green pepper, seeded and diced
½ cup crushed ice

Cut smoked salmon into ¼-inch by 3-inch strips. (If using salted salmon, soak in cold water overnight, and rinse thoroughly.) Combine the salmon with tomatoes, scallions, and green peppers; mix thoroughly. Spoon into a glass bowl, stir in the ice, and serve at once. Makes 4 to 6 servings.

Hungarian Potato Salad

½ teaspoon dry mustard
½ teaspoon warm water
4 cups diced cooked potato
3 tablespoons chopped green onion
½ cup diced peeled cucumber
½ cup diced radishes
4 hard-cooked eggs
1 cup dairy sour cream
2 teaspoons paprika
1 tablespoon cider vinegar
1¼ teaspoons salt
1 teaspoon celery seed
1 teaspoon poppy seed
Lettuce

Mix mustard with the warm water and let stand 10 minutes for flavor to develop. In large salad bowl, combine potato, onion, cucumber, and radishes; set aside.

Separate egg yolks from whites. Dice whites and add to potato mixture. In small bowl, mash yolks and stir in mustard, sour cream, paprika, vinegar, salt, celery seed and poppy seed. Add to salad and mix well. Chill thoroughly. Serve on lettuce and sprinkle with paprika. Makes 6 to 8 servings.

Gado Gado (Indonesian Vegetable Salad with Spicy Peanut Sauce)

    3 peeled carrots, cut into matchsticks
    ½ pound fresh green beans, cut in thin
          diagonals
      Salt
    3 medium potatoes, cooked, peeled, and
          diced
    4 cups shredded salad greens (lettuce, kale,
          spinach, escarole, or chicory)
    1 can (1 pound) bean sprouts, drained, or 1
          pound fresh bean sprouts
    1 tomato, cut in wedges
    3 hard-cooked eggs, quartered
      Peanut Sauce*

Steam carrots and beans separately in small amounts of salted water until crisp-tender; drain, reserving liquid for peanut sauce. If using canned sprouts, drain and rinse them in cold water; if using fresh sprouts, put them in boiling water for 1 minute and drain them. Chill vegetables. Spread greens on large platter. Arrange carrots, potatoes, green beans and bean sprouts in rows. Garnish with tomato wedges and egg quarters. Chill until serving time. Serve with peanut sauce. Makes 6 servings.

Italian Pepper and Cheese Salad

    3 to 4 sweet red peppers
    6 cups mixed shredded salad greens
    6 scallions, chopped
    ½ cup chopped celery
    6 anchovy fillets, cut up
    ¾ pound fontina cheese, cubed
    ½ cup Italian Dressing*

Using a long-handled fork, heat the peppers over a gas flame or bake them in a 400°F oven until the skins are black and blistered. Rub the skins off under cold running water. Remove seeds and slice the peppers. Place the lettuce, scallions, celery, and anchovies in a salad bowl and toss together. Arrange the peppers around the bowl in spoke-like fashion and place the cheese cubes in the center. Pour the dressing over the salad and toss. Makes 6 servings.

Tabbouleh (Iranian Cracked Wheat Salad)

    1 cup fine cracked wheat (bulgur)
    2 large ripe tomatoes, peeled, seeded, and
        diced
    1 medium cucumber, peeled, seeded, and
        diced
    1 medium green pepper, seeded and chopped
    ½ cup chopped onion
    ½ cup chopped parsley
    2 tablespoons minced chives
    ½ cup chopped fresh mint or 2 tablespoons
        dried

½ cup olive oil
¼ cup lemon juice
1 teaspoon salt
¼ teaspoon freshly ground pepper
Salad greens

Soak the bulgur for half an hour in cold water to cover. Drain, dry thoroughly, and put the wheat in a bowl. Add tomatoes, cucumbers, green pepper, onion, parsley, chives, and mint. Mix well. Combine the oil, lemon juice, salt, and pepper and pour over the salad. Toss thoroughly. Place on a serving platter surrounded by greens. Makes 6 servings.

Japanese Soy, Beef, and Green Salad

½ pound round or lean chuck steak, about
    ½-inch thick
⅓ cup soy sauce
1 clove garlic, mashed
½ cup plus 2 tablespoons oil
3 cups torn spinach leaves (about ½ pound)
3 cups torn salad greens (romaine, Boston,
    Bibb, or iceberg)
1 cup bean sprouts
3 tablespoons lemon juice
½ teaspoon salt
¼ teaspoon freshly ground pepper
½ cup chopped peanuts

Partially freeze meat and slice paper-thin. Toss with soy sauce. Brown garlic in 2 tablespoons hot oil and remove it. Sauté beef strips a few at a time for less than a minute, turning to brown evenly; remove, cover, and chill. In a salad bowl toss spinach, greens, sprouts, remaining oil, the lemon juice, salt, and pepper. Arrange meat strips in center of the greens and sprinkle with peanuts. Makes 4 servings.

Mexican Guacamole

   2 large ripe avocados, well mashed
  ½ cup canned chopped green chili peppers
   1 large tomato, peeled, chopped, and drained
  ½ teaspoon salt
   1 tablespoon Worcestershire sauce
   2 tablespoons grated onion
   2 tablespoons lemon juice

Mix avocado, chili peppers, tomato, salt, Worcestershire sauce, and onion with half the lemon juice and spoon into a serving bowl. Sprinkle with remaining lemon juice to prevent discoloration, cover with plastic wrap, and chill. Serve as a canapé with crisp taco chips. Serves 8 to 10.

Taco Salad

   1 pound ground beef
   1 tablespoon oil
   1 can (1 pound) stewed tomatoes
  ¼ cup canned taco sauce
    Salt
    Freshly ground pepper
   1 medium head iceberg lettuce
  ½ cup chopped onion
  ½ cup shredded Cheddar cheese
   6 ounces corn chips

Brown meat in oil in the skillet and drain off fat. Add liquid from tomatoes and taco sauce and simmer 5 minutes. Season to taste with salt and pepper and set aside to cool. Tear lettuce in bite-size pieces in a large bowl. Add reserved tomatoes and meat mixture. Top with chopped onion, cheese, and corn chips. Serve at once. Makes 4 to 6 servings.

Panamanian Radish Salad

   3 bunches radishes
   ½ cup thin sweet onion rings
   1 cup peeled diced fresh tomato
   1 teaspoon salt
   ¼ teaspoon freshly ground pepper
   2 teaspoons finely chopped fresh mint
   2 tablespoons lemon juice
   2 tablespoons salad oil
     Parsley

Wash, trim, and slice radishes. Add onion and tomato. Combine the salt, pepper, mint, lemon juice, and oil; mix well and pour over the salad. Toss lightly. Garnish with parsley. Makes 6 servings.

New Zealand Sardine Salad

    1 can (8 to 9 ounces) medium sardines
    ⅓ cup salad oil
    ¼ cup vinegar
    ½ teaspoon salt
    ⅛ teaspoon freshly ground pepper
    1 hard-cooked egg, chopped
    3 cups cooked diced potatoes
    ¼ cup chopped parsley
    1 green pepper, chopped
    1 small onion, chopped
    1 large cucumber, peeled and diced
      Lettuce
    1 hard-cooked egg, sliced
      Pimiento-stuffed olives

Cut half the sardines into ½-inch pieces; reserve remainder. Mix oil, vinegar, salt, pepper, and chopped egg. Place cut sardines, potatoes, parsley, green pepper, onion, and cucumber in a bowl and toss with the dressing. Arrange salad on lettuce-lined platter. Garnish with reserved whole sardines, egg slices, and olives. Makes 6 servings.

Polish Potato Salad

    6 large potatoes, cooked, peeled, and sliced thin
    2 large onions, sliced thin
    2 sweet pickles, chopped
    1 cup diced celery
    1 teaspoon salt
    ¼ teaspoon freshly ground pepper
    6 slices bacon, diced

2 tablespoons flour
¼ cup hot water
¼ cup white vinegar
2 tablespoons olive oil
1 tablespoon sugar
2 tablespoons chopped parsley

Combine potatoes with the onions, pickles, celery, salt, and pepper. Sauté the bacon until crisp; remove the pieces with a slotted spoon and add to the potato mixture. Heat 2 tablespoons bacon drippings in pan; stir in the flour and blend well. Add the water slowly while stirring. Add vinegar, oil, and sugar and bring to a boil. Remove from heat and cool the sauce slightly. Pour sauce over the potatoes, toss gently, and sprinkle with parsley. Serve warm or cold. Makes 6 servings.

Russian Salad

3 medium potatoes, cooked, peeled, and cubed
1 cup cooked small peas
1 package (10 ounces) frozen cut green beans,
    cooked and drained
1 cup cooked diced carrots
1 cup cooked diced beets
1 can (2½ ounces) sliced mushrooms, drained
½ cup pimiento-stuffed olives, sliced
1 sweet onion, chopped fine
2 tablespoons wine vinegar
1 teaspoon salt
½ teaspoon white pepper
2 tablespoons chopped parsley
½ cup Mayonnaise*
2 tablespoons vodka
  Crisp lettuce cups

Cover and chill potatoes. Place them in a wide salad bowl with the peas, beans, carrots, beets, mushrooms, and olives. Mix onion, vinegar, salt, pepper, and parsley and beat with the mayonnaise and vodka. Pour over salad and toss thoroughly. Refrigerate until ready to serve. Spoon into lettuce cups. Makes 8 servings.

Scandinavian Herring and Beet Salad

1 jar (6 ounces) herring, drained and diced
1 tablespoon juice from the herring
6 small beets, quartered
2 tablespoons beet juice
3 cooked potatoes, peeled and diced
3 dill pickles, diced
½ cup Mayonnaise*
½ cup dairy sour cream
1 teaspoon sugar
  Salad greens

Mix the herring, beets, potatoes, and pickles in a bowl. Combine the mayonnaise, sour cream, and sugar with 1 tablespoon juice from the herring and 2 tablespoons beet juice. Pour over the salad and mix very thoroughly. Chill for several hours. Turn out on a platter and garnish with greens. Makes 6 servings.

Swedish Cucumbers

       3 large cucumbers, peeled and sliced thin
       2 tablespoons coarse salt
     ¼ cup white vinegar
       1 tablespoon sugar
     ½ teaspoon white pepper
       1 teaspoon dried or 1 tablespoon minced fresh
              dill

Layer the cucumbers and salt in a bowl. Cover and refrigerate for several hours. Rinse cucumbers in a strainer under cold water; drain and dry. Combine vinegar, sugar, pepper, and dill and pour over the cucumbers. Toss and taste for seasoning. Makes 6 servings.

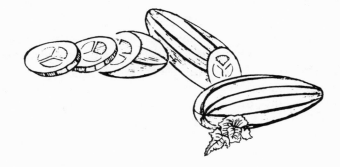

FOUR

The Meal Salad
nutritious and satisfying

You don't have to be on a diet to eat a salad as a main course. After a brisk game of tennis, a "chef's salad," probably America's most popular main course salad, is an ideal entrée. Traditionally, it includes ham, chicken, and Swiss cheese cut in julienne strips and served in a bowl of greens with a favorite dressing.

For an after-theater supper, make a colorful platter salad, refrigerate it while you go out, and return to a delicious ready-to-eat meal. Treat your guests to mounds of shrimp and chicken salads alternating with sliced or stuffed tomatoes, avocado, shredded carrots, cheese, crisp greens, rolled cold cuts, and a choice of dressings.

Main course salads are economical protein-stretchers that also provide vitamins, minerals, and fiber—essential for a healthy, balanced, and satisfying meal.

Chef's Salad

        4 cups assorted salad greens, torn into
              bite-size pieces
        1 cup ham, cut in julienne strips
        1 cup cooked chicken, cut in julienne strips
        1 cup Swiss cheese, cut in julienne strips
       12 tomato wedges
        1 can (2 ounces) anchovies, drained (optional)
        ½ to ¾ cup French Dressing*

102

Place the greens in a serving salad bowl. Top with the ham, chicken, and cheese. Arrange the tomatoes around the edge of the bowl and garnish with anchovies, if you wish. Add the dressing and toss at the table. Makes 6 servings.

VARIATIONS

I. Substitute tongue or corned beef for the ham in Chef's Salad.*
II. Substitute turkey for the chicken in Chef's Salad.*
III. Substitute Bel Paese, Gruyère, or Muenster cheese for the Swiss cheese in Chef's Salad.*
IV. Substitute Roquefort* or Blue Cheese* or Thousand Island Dressing* for French Dressing* in Chef's Salad.*

Cobb Salad

6 cups torn salad greens (lettuce, chicory, romaine, escarole)
½ bunch watercress, leaves only
1 avocado, peeled and diced
1 teaspoon lemon juice
2 large tomatoes, peeled and coarsely chopped
2 tablespoons minced chives
3 hard-cooked eggs, chopped
6 slices bacon, fried crisp and crumbled
2 cups cooked chicken, diced
1 package (4 ounces) blue cheese, crumbled
1 cup Lemon French Dressing*

Mix the salad greens and combine with the watercress leaves. Line a deep platter with the greens. Sprinkle the avocado with lemon juice as you dice it, to prevent discoloration. Arrange a row of tomatoes down the center of the platter and sprinkle with the chives. Make rows of the eggs, bacon, chicken, and avocado down the sides. Crumble the cheese over the salad and serve with dressing. Makes 6 servings.

Fish-Vegetable Salad

    4 green peppers, cut into 1-inch pieces
    2 ribs celery, cut into ½-inch slices
    3 scallions, sliced thin
    1 carrot, sliced thin
    1 zucchini, sliced thin
    ½ cup pitted black olives
    ⅓ cup oil
    ¼ cup lemon juice
    1 teaspoon salt
      Freshly ground pepper to taste
1½ pounds fish fillets (cod, turbot, or haddock),
          poached, chilled, and flaked
      Salad greens
    2 tomatoes, peeled and cut into wedges
    3 tablespoons minced parsley

In a large mixing bowl combine green peppers, celery, scallions, carrot, zucchini, olives, oil, lemon juice, salt, and pepper, and mix thoroughly. Gently stir in fish. Arrange greens on a serving platter and spoon fish mixture in center. Garnish with tomato wedges and parsley. Makes 6 servings.

Salade Niçoise

        5 small new potatoes
          Boiling salted water
        2 cups green beans, crisp-cooked
          Romaine lettuce
        1 small green pepper, sliced in very thin rings
        1 sweet red onion, sliced and separated
        1 can (2 ounces) flat anchovy fillets, drained
            and chopped
        1 can (6½ or 7 ounces) tuna
        3 firm tomatoes, cut in wedges
        3 hard-cooked eggs, quartered
        1 dozen black olives
          Freshly ground pepper
        1 cup Vinaigrette Dressing*

Cook potatoes in small amount of boiling salted water until just tender; peel and dice while warm. Toss with about 4 tablespoons dressing and chill. Toss well-drained beans with a little dressing and chill. At serving time, heap potatoes in small mound on large serving plate or shallow bowl ringed with romaine. Combine green beans, pepper rings, onion and anchovies with about half the remaining dressing. Toss gently and heap mixture around the potato salad. Garnish salad with chunks of tuna, tomatoes, eggs, and olives. Sprinkle with salt and pepper. Pour on remaining dressing. Makes 4 to 6 servings.

Salmon Salad

    2 cans (7½ ounces each) red salmon, drained
      and flaked
    2 medium tomatoes, peeled and chopped
    2 small cucumbers, peeled and chopped
    ½ cup yogurt
    6 tablespoons Lemon French Dressing*
    1 tablespoon fresh dill or 1 teaspoon dried
      Lettuce

Mix salmon with the tomatoes and cucumbers. Combine
the yogurt with the dressing and dill and stir it into the
salmon mixture. Serve chilled on a lettuce-lined plate.
Makes 4 servings.

Egg-Sardine Platter

      Romaine lettuce, torn into bite-size pieces
    4 hard-cooked eggs, quartered
    1 can (9 ounces) boned skinned sardines,
      drained
    1 tablespoon lemon juice
    2 tablespoons minced scallions
      Salt
      Freshly ground pepper
    ⅓ cup croutons
    ⅓ cup Caesar Dressing *

Line a serving dish with the romaine lettuce. Arrange
eggs and sardines on the greens. Sprinkle with lemon
juice, scallions, and salt and pepper to taste. Just before
serving, toss croutons with the dressing. Pour over the
salad and serve at once. Makes 2 to 4 servings.

Shrimp Salad

 1½ pounds small shrimp, peeled, cooked, and
     chilled
 1 small onion, chopped fine
 2 tablespoons minced parsley
 ½ cup pimiento-stuffed olives, sliced
 3 hard-cooked eggs, coarsely chopped
 ½ cup Mayonnaise*
 ¼ cup dairy sour cream
 2 teaspoons lemon juice
   Lettuce
 6 anchovy fillets (optional)

Combine the shrimp with the onion, parsley, olives, and
hard-cooked eggs. Mix the mayonnaise with sour cream
and lemon juice. Pour over the salad and toss. Serve on
shredded lettuce or in crisp lettuce cups. Garnish with
anchovy fillets, if you wish. Makes 6 servings.

Shrimp and Tomato Salad

 1½ pounds shrimp, peeled, cooked, and chilled
 2 large tomatoes, peeled and coarsely chopped
 1 cup diced celery
 1 tablespoon capers
 1 teaspoon lemon juice
 ½ cup Louis Dressing*

Cut the shrimp in half lengthwise; if large cut once again
crosswise. Combine with the tomatoes, celery, and capers. Add lemon juice to the Louis dressing, pour over the
salad, and toss. Spoon onto individual plates. Makes 4 to
6 servings.

Tuna Salad

    2 cans (9 ounces each) tuna
    1 cup chopped celery
    3 hard-cooked eggs, coarsely chopped
    2 tablespoons chopped parsley
    ½ cup Mayonnaise*
    3 tablespoons lemon juice
    ¼ teaspoon freshly ground pepper
      Shredded lettuce

Drain the tuna and flake, reserving the liquid. Combine tuna, celery, eggs, and parsley. Blend the mayonnaise with lemon juice, pepper, and the liquid from the tuna. Toss together gently and chill. Serve on shredded lettuce. Makes 6 servings.

Tuna-Cranberry Salad

    2 cups cranberries
    1 cup sugar
    ⅓ cup water
    2 cans (6½ or 7 ounces each) tuna in oil
    ⅓ cup vinegar
    2 teaspoons celery seed
    ½ teaspoon salt
      Salad oil
    3 cups torn raw spinach leaves
    3 cups torn lettuce leaves
 1½ cups orange chunks

Bring cranberries, sugar, and ⅓ cup water to brisk boil. Remove from heat and cool. Drain off syrup and reserve ⅓ cup. Chill berries. Drain oil from tuna into measuring cup; break tuna in chunks. Combine cranberry syrup, vinegar, celery seed, and salt. Add enough salad oil to tuna oil to make ⅔ cup. Add to cranberry syrup/vinegar mixture and beat until blended. Put spinach and lettuce in a large glass bowl. Arrange tuna, cranberries, and oranges on top; pour dressing over salad and toss lightly. Serve at once. Makes 6 to 8 servings.

Chicken Avocado Salad

    3 cups diced cooked chicken
    1 cup chopped celery
    1 cup Mayonnaise*
    3 tablespoons lemon juice
    1 teaspoon salt
    ¼ teaspoon freshly ground pepper
    2 ripe avocados, peeled and diced
      Mixed salad greens

In a bowl combine chicken, celery, mayonnaise, lemon juice, salt, and pepper. Mix well. Gently toss with the diced avocado. Taste for seasoning. Serve on platter surrounded with mixed greens. Makes 6 servings.

Mimosa Chicken Salad

 2 cups diced cooked chicken
 1 cucumber, peeled, cut in half lengthwise,
   seeded, and sliced
 ½ green pepper, cut in fine strips
 ½ cup creamed cottage cheese
 ½ cup buttermilk
 1 teaspoon prepared mustard
 2 tablespoons minced green onion
 ¾ teaspoon salt
  Freshly ground pepper
  Lettuce
 1 hard-cooked egg, sieved

Combine chicken, cucumber, and green pepper. Whirl cottage cheese and buttermilk in blender or beat until smooth. Add mustard, onion, salt, and pepper and mix until well blended. Pour over chicken mixture and toss thoroughly. Spoon into lettuce-lined serving dish. Garnish with egg. Makes 4 servings.

Chicken-Pineapple Salad

 3 cups diced cooked chicken
 1 can (13¼ ounces) pineapple tidbits, drained
 2 tablespoons sliced green onion
 1 can (6 ounces) water chestnuts, drained and slivered
 ½ cup Mayonnaise*
 ½ cup dairy sour cream
 ½ teaspoon salt
 ½ teaspoon ground ginger
 ¼ teaspoon freshly ground pepper
 ¼ cup toasted slivered almonds
  Salad greens or sprigs of watercress

Combine chicken, pineapple, onion, and water chestnuts and chill. Blend mayonnaise and sour cream with salt, ginger, and pepper and add to chicken mixture. Toss and sprinkle with almonds. Serve on greens or garnish with sprigs of watercress. Makes 6 servings.

Hot Chicken-Rice Salad

        1 cup cooked rice
        2 cups diced cooked chicken
      ¼ cup sliced pimiento-stuffed olives
        1 cup sliced celery
        2 tablespoons chopped chives or green onions
      ¾ cup Mayonnaise*
          Salt
          Freshly ground pepper
      ¼ cup coarsely chopped almonds

Place the rice in a bowl, add chicken, olives, celery, chives, and mayonnaise and mix lightly. Season to taste. Turn into shallow 1½ quart baking dish and sprinkle with the almonds. Bake in preheated 375°F oven 20 minutes or until heated. Sprinkle with minced parsley if desired. Makes 4 servings. NOTE: Serve leftovers cold.

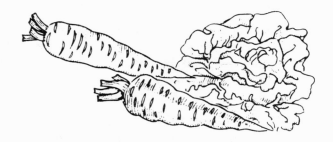

Special Chicken Salad

    1 package (10 ounces) fresh spinach
    3 cups diced cooked chicken, chilled
    ¾ cup chopped walnuts
    2 apples, cored and chopped
    ½ cup salad oil
    ¼ cup red wine vinegar
    1 tablespoon chopped chives
    ½ teaspoon salt
    ⅛ teaspoon freshly ground pepper
    1 teaspoon sugar

Wash and dry spinach; discard stems and tear into bite-size pieces. Add chicken, walnuts, and apples. Mix salad oil with vinegar, chives, salt, pepper, and sugar; toss lightly with salad. Attractive served in a large glass bowl. Makes 6 servings.

Turkey Salad Platter

    1 package (10 ounces) frozen french-cut green
        beans, cooked and drained
    1 teaspoon vinegar
    ½ teaspoon dried summer savory or dillweed
    3 cups lettuce leaves, washed and torn into
        small pieces
    2 cups cooked turkey, cut into julienne strips
    2 tomatoes, cut in eighths
    1 cucumber unpeeled and sliced thin
    1½ cups Thousand Island Dressing*

In small bowl toss beans with vinegar and savory or dillweed; chill. Line a large platter with lettuce and arrange the turkey, tomatoes, cucumber, and beans in attractive mounds. Spoon half the dressing over the salad and serve the remainder in a pitcher. Makes 6 servings.

Turkey-Chutney Salad

　½ cup chutney
　½ cup Mayonnaise*
　½ teaspoon salt
　2 cups cooked turkey, cut into julienne strips
1½ cups pineapple chunks, drained
　1 can (8 ounces) water chestnuts, drained and
　　　sliced
　¼ cup chopped green pepper
　　Lettuce
　　Fresh coconut, grated (optional)

Mix well chutney, mayonnaise, and salt. Gently stir in turkey, pineapple water chestnuts, and green pepper. Blend until ingredients are well coated. Chill at least one hour. Serve on lettuce with a sprinkling of fresh coconut. Makes 4 to 6 servings.

Fresh Mushroom-Turkey Salad

　½ pound mushrooms, sliced thin
　3 cups diced cooked turkey
　1 cup diced celery
　¼ cup thinly sliced radishes
　2 tablespoons minced scallions
　2 tablespoons chopped parsley
　5 tablespoons lemon juice
　⅔ cup olive oil
　¾ teaspoon salt
　　Freshly ground pepper
　　Lettuce cups

In mixing bowl, toss mushrooms with the turkey, celery, radishes, scallions, and parsley. Blend lemon juice, oil, salt, and pepper and add to the turkey mixture. Toss lightly and chill. Serve in crisp lettuce cups. Makes 6 servings.

Turkey-Pear Salad

>   2 cups diced cooked turkey
>   2 cups diced fresh pears (unpeeled if
>   preferred)
>   1 to 2 teaspoons curry powder
>   ¼ cup water
>   ½ cup coarsely chopped toasted pecans
>   ½ cup Mayonnaise*
>   ¼ cup milk
>   Salt
>   Freshly ground pepper
>   Tomato wedges

Combine turkey and pears in mixing bowl. Mix curry powder with the water in small saucepan. Heat gently 1 minute. Add to turkey mixture with combined pecans, mayonnaise, and milk and mix well. Season with salt and pepper. Put in serving dish and arrange tomato wedges around edge. Makes 4 servings.

Beef Salad

>   3 cups cooked beef, cut into ½-inch cubes
>   1½ cups chopped celery
>   1 cup chopped scallions
>   1 cup chopped green pepper

2 large tomatoes, peeled and diced
1 teaspoon prepared mustard
1 cup French Dressing*
  Watercress
  Minced parsley

Combine the beef, celery, scallions, green pepper, and tomatoes in a bowl. Add the mustard to the dressing. Pour over the salad and toss thoroughly. Serve on watercress and garnish with minced parsley. Makes 6 servings.

Beef-Mushroom Salad

½ cup oil
¼ cup cider vinegar
1 tablespoon soy sauce
¼ cup minced parsley
2 green onions, minced
½ teaspoon salt
¼ teaspoon freshly ground pepper
½ pound mushrooms, sliced thin
2 cups thin slices cooked steak, roast beef, or
    beef pot roast
4 cups torn salad greens

In salad bowl blend oil, vinegar, soy sauce, parsley, onions, salt, and pepper. Add mushrooms and meat and toss to coat; marinate at room temperature at least ½ hour. Just before serving add greens and toss. Makes 4 to 6 servings.

Ham-Vegetable Salad

             1 to 2 cups diced cooked ham
             2 pounds fresh green beans, cooked
             1 can (1 pound) kidney beans, drained
             1 or 2 fresh tomatoes, diced
             1 cup cooked white rice
            ½ cup cooked sliced carrots
            ¼ cup vegetable oil
             3 tablespoons cider vinegar
             1 teaspoon salt
            ¼ teaspoon freshly ground pepper
             1 tablespoon each minced onion, parsley, and
                    green pepper
             1 tablespoon pickle relish

In large bowl combine ham, green beans, kidney beans, tomatoes, rice, and carrots. Mix together oil, vinegar, salt, pepper, onion, parsley, green pepper, and pickle relish, pour over salad and toss. Chill thoroughly. Makes 6 servings.

Meat-Rice Salad Platter

            ½ cup French Dressing*
             1 teaspoon paprika
            ¼ teaspoon dry mustard
            ½ teaspoon curry powder
                 Pinch of tarragon
          1½ cups diced cooked pork, veal, beef, or
                    chicken
             3 cups cooked white rice
             1 cup sliced radishes
                 Salt

      Freshly ground pepper
1   cup coarsely shredded carrot
1   cup coarsely shredded white turnip
      Mayonnaise* or Green-Goddess Dressing*
      Sliced scored cucumbers
2   tomatoes, sliced
      Green-pepper strips
      Finely sliced green onion
      Black and pimiento-stuffed olives
      Watercress
      Pimiento rose

Whip together dressing, paprika, mustard, curry, and tarragon. Mix with diced meat and rice and chill until serving time. Stir in radishes and season to taste with salt and pepper. Pile in center of serving plate and surround with individual mounds of carrot and turnip each mixed with a little mayonnaise or green-goddess dressing. Garnish with cucumbers, tomatoes, green peppers, onions, olives, watercress, and pimiento. Makes 6 to 8 servings.

Cabbage-Potato-Meat Salad

        2 large cooked potatoes, peeled and cut into
               ½-inch cubes
        2 cups finely shredded red or green cabbage
        1 can (7 ounces) luncheon meat, chilled and
               cut into ½-inch cubes
       ¼ cup chopped green onion
       ¼ cup chopped dill pickle
       ¾ cup Mayonnaise*
       ¼ cup milk
        2 tablespoons cider vinegar
       ½ teaspoon celery seed
       ½ teaspoon mustard seed
       ½ teaspoon salt
        1 to 2 teaspoons sugar
           Salad greens
        3 hard-cooked eggs, halved
           Radishes

Combine potatoes, cabbage, meat, onion, and pickle in
large mixing bowl. In a separate bowl mix well mayonnaise, milk, vinegar, celery and mustard seed, salt, and
sugar. Pour over potato mixture and toss. Line platter
with greens and pile salad in center. Arrange eggs and
radishes around edge. Makes 4 servings.

Potato Salad with Ham and Green Beans

       ⅔ cup oil
        6 tablespoons cider vinegar
        3 tablespoons chopped parsley
        3 tablespoons chopped green onion

½ teaspoon salt
Freshly ground pepper
5 medium potatoes, cooked and sliced
1 pound green beans, cooked
½ cup thinly sliced radishes
2 cups chopped watercress leaves
2 cups slivered ham

Combine oil, vinegar, parsley, onion, salt, and pepper. In bowl layer warm potato slices and half the dressing; cover and let stand at room temperature at least 30 minutes. To assemble salad, place beans mixed with radishes in the bottom of a glass bowl. Dribble with most of remaining dressing. Layer the potatoes over the beans; add half of the watercress. Top with the ham and remaining watercress. Pour any remaining dressing over salad and toss to mix. Makes 6 servings.

Smoked Tongue Salad

⅓ cup Mayonnaise*
¼ cup oil
3 teaspoons prepared horseradish
3 tablespoons cider vinegar
½ teaspoon salt
½ teaspoon freshly ground pepper
3 cups smoked tongue, cut into julienne strips
5 medium potatoes, cooked, peeled, and
    cubed
1 package (10 ounces) frozen peas, cooked
    and cooled
2 ribs celery, scraped and sliced thin
  Salad greens

In a large bowl blend mayonnaise, oil, horseradish, vinegar, salt, and pepper. Add tongue, potatoes, peas, and celery; toss gently. Serve chilled on a bed of greens. Makes 8 servings.

Sunset Salad

> 2 cups shredded cabbage
> 2 cups smoked tongue, cut into julienne strips
> 2 cups cooked chicken, cut into julienne strips
> 1 cup Lorenzo Dressing*

Combine the cabbage, tongue, and chicken in a mixing bowl. Pour the dressing over the salad and toss well. Makes 6 to 8 servings.

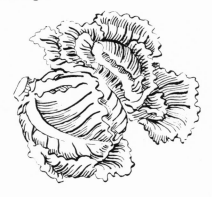

FIVE

Hearty, Filling Salads

macaroni, rice, and potato salads

Whether you cook for one or twenty, you will welcome salads of macaroni, rice, and potatoes to serve after a busy day in the office or at home. Prepared in advance, these easy economical dishes keep well in the refrigerator for several days.

Perfect with light entrées, such as cold cuts, baked ham, or crisp barbecued chicken, they are the most portable of salads. Take along containers of curried potato salad or rice with crab meat on your next weekend trip to the country or the beach and enjoy extra time running, swimming, or relaxing.

Macaroni Salad

  1 pound elbow macaroni or shells
  4 hard-cooked eggs, diced
  1 large red or Bermuda onion, sliced thin
  1 cup Mayonnaise*
 ¼ cup heavy cream
  1 teaspoon salt
 ¼ teaspoon freshly ground pepper
  1 teaspoon dill
  6 strips bacon, cooked

Cook the macaroni according to package instructions and drain. Combine it with the eggs, onion, mayonnaise,

121

cream, salt, pepper, and dill; toss well. Cover and chill. Cook the bacon until crisp, dry on paper towel, and crumble. Sprinkle over the salad just before serving. Makes 6 servings.

Macaroni and Bean Salad

    2 cups elbow macaroni
    1 can (1 pound) red kidney beans, drained
    ½ cup Mayonnaise*
    ¼ cup French Dressing*
       Dash of hot pepper sauce
    ⅓ cup diced sweet pickles
    2 tablespoons cider vinegar
    6 hard-cooked eggs, diced
       Salt
       Freshly ground pepper
       Watercress or mixed salad greens

Cook macaroni, drain, and cool slightly. Combine in a bowl with the beans. Mix the mayonnaise, dressing, hot pepper sauce, pickles, and vinegar; toss with macaroni. Fold in eggs and mix carefully. Add salt and pepper to taste. Serve chilled on a platter of watercress or mixed greens. Makes 8 servings.

Macaroni-Cabbage Salad

    1½ cups elbow macaroni, cooked, drained, and
          cooled
    1 medium green pepper, cut into julienne
          strips
    1 small onion, minced

1 large carrot, shredded
4 cups shredded red or green cabbage
1 tablespoon prepared mustard
1 cup Mayonnaise*
½ cup light cream
½ teaspoon salt
¼ teaspoon freshly ground pepper

Combine the macaroni with green pepper, onion, carrot, and cabbage in a large mixing bowl. Stir together mustard, mayonnaise, cream, salt, and pepper, and pour over macaroni mixture. Toss and chill at least one hour before serving. Makes 8 servings.

Macaroni and Cheese Salad

2 cups elbow macaroni
1 cup diced cooked smoked tongue or corned
    beef
1 cup thinly sliced celery
1 cup shredded sharp Cheddar cheese
1 cup sliced pimiento-stuffed olives
1 small green pepper, slivered
¼ cup minced red onion
1 cup Russian Dressing*
  Lettuce

Cook macaroni according to directions on package. Drain, cool, and combine with diced meat, celery, cheese, olives, green pepper, and onion. Toss gently with dressing and serve on crisp lettuce. Makes 6 to 8 servings.

Seashell Clam Salad

    1½ cups small shell macaroni
    1 can (8 ounces) minced clams, drained
    ½ cup chopped black olives
    ½ cup chopped celery
    ¼ cup chopped parsley
    2 tablespoons white-wine vinegar
    ½ cup vegetable oil
    1 teaspoon salt
      Freshly ground black pepper
    1 small clove garlic, minced
      Tomato wedges or slices

Cook and drain macaroni according to package directions. Combine in large mixing bowl with clams, olives, celery, and parsley. Mix together vinegar, oil, salt, pepper, and garlic and pour over salad. Toss and marinate at least ½ hour before serving. Garnish with tomatoes. Makes 4 to 6 servings.

Crab-Meat Macaroni Salad

    3 cans (6½ ounces each) crab meat, drained
      and flaked
    2 cups elbow macaroni
    1 cucumber, peeled, seeded, and diced
    1 tablespoon grated onion
    1 cup Mayonnaise*
    2 tablespoons French Dressing*
    1 teaspoon lemon juice
    ½ teaspoon salt
      Minced parsley

Cook, drain, and cool macaroni according to package directions. Drain the crab meat and reserve the juice. Combine the macaroni with the crab meat, cucumber, and onion. Blend the mayonnaise with the dressing, liquid from the crab meat, lemon juice, and salt. Pour over the salad and toss thoroughly. Chill. Garnish with minced parsley. Makes 6 to 8 servings.

Macaroni Salad with Ham

    12 ounces elbow macaroni
      2 cups diced cooked ham
    ¼ cup minced scallions or shallots
      2 teaspoons prepared mustard
    ½ teaspoon salt
    ½ cup French Dressing*
    ½ cup Mayonnaise*
      2 tablespoons cut-up pimientos
      3 tablespoons minced parsley

Cook the macaroni according to package directions; drain and cool. Add the ham and scallions or shallots to the macaroni. Combine the mustard and salt with the dressing and mayonnaise and mix thoroughly into the salad. Chill for several hours. Serve garnished with pimientos and minced parsley. Makes 6 servings.

Marinated Macaroni Salad with Watercress

    1½ cups elbow macaroni
     1 teaspoon prepared mustard
     2 tablespoons wine vinegar
     6 tablespoons vegetable oil
    ½ teaspoon salt
       Freshly ground black pepper
     1 cup thinly sliced celery
    ¼ cup chopped green onions
     1 cup chopped watercress
    ½ cup Mayonnaise*
    ½ cup milk
    ½ cup sliced radishes
       Watercress sprigs

Cook and drain macaroni according to package directions. Put in large mixing bowl. Combine mustard, vinegar, oil, ½ teaspoon salt and pepper to taste. Pour over
macaroni and toss. Cover and marinate several hours or
overnight. Add celery, green onions, watercress, and
mayonnaise blended with milk. Mix lightly and correct
seasoning. Pour into serving dish and garnish with
radishes and watercress sprigs. Makes 6 servings.

Apple-Raisin-Rice Salad

     1 cup rice
    ½ cup golden raisins
     2 tablespoons vinegar
    ¼ cup salad oil
     1 teaspoon thyme leaves, crumbled

1 large eating apple, cored and slivered
      (peeled, if desired)
2 tablespoons lemon juice
⅔ cup chopped black olives
   Salt
1 cup diced sharp Cheddar or Gruyère cheese

Cook rice according to package directions. Soak raisins in
boiling water 5 minutes; drain. Mix rice and raisins with
combined vinegar, oil, and thyme. Sprinkle apples with
lemon juice and stir gently into rice mixture. Add olives,
season with salt to taste, and chill. Just before serving add
cheese. Makes 6 servings.

Beet and Rice Salad

2 cups diced canned beets, drained
2 cups cooked rice
¼ cup chopped scallions
½ cup Lemon French Dressing*
2 tablespoons dairy sour cream or
      Mayonnaise*
2 tablespoons minced parsley
   Romaine lettuce

Put the beets, rice, and scallions in a bowl. Combine the
dressing with the sour cream or mayonnaise and the
parsley. Pour over the beet-rice mixture and toss
thoroughly. Refrigerate for several hours. Serve on a
platter ringed with romaine. Makes 4 servings.

Peanutty Carrot and Brown-Rice Salad

    1 cup peanut butter
    2 tablespoons honey
    4 cups cooked brown rice
    2 cups shredded carrots
    1 teaspoon salt
    ¼ teaspoon freshly ground pepper
      Lettuce leaves
      Cucumber and tomato slices

In large bowl stir together peanut butter and honey. Add rice, carrots, salt, and pepper; stir until well mixed. Chill well. Serve on a bed of lettuce garnished with cucumber and tomato slices. Makes 8 servings.

Soy Brown Rice Salad

    1 cup uncooked brown rice
      Cold-pressed corn or safflower oil
    2 cups water
      Salt
    2 cups coarsely shredded carrot
    ½ cup thinly sliced celery
    1 green pepper, cut into thin 2-inch strips
    3 green onions, thinly sliced
    1 cup peas, cooked
    2 pimientos, diced
    ½ cup salted roasted soy beans
    ¾ cup Lemon French Dressing*
      Salt
      Freshly ground pepper

Put rice in heavy saucepan and add about 1 teaspoon oil. Heat, stirring, until rice is lightly browned. (This step cuts down on cooking time.) Cool slightly, add 2 cups water and 1 teaspoon salt. Bring to boil, cover, and simmer 30 minutes, or until tender. Cool to room temperature. Add carrots, celery, green pepper, onions, peas, pimientos, soy beans, dressing, and salt and pepper to taste. Chill. Makes 6 to 8 servings.

Brown-Rice Vegetable Salad

   3 cups cooked brown rice, cooled
  ¾ cup coarsely shredded carrot
  ¾ cup coarsely shredded zucchini
   3 tablespoons chopped parsley
   2 tablespoons finely chopped onion
  ½ cup Lemon French Dressing*
  ½ teaspoon thyme
  ¼ teaspoon salt

In a large bowl mix rice, carrots, zucchini, parsley, and onion. Combine dressing with salt and thyme; pour over salad and toss well. Refrigerate several hours or overnight. Makes 6 to 8 servings.

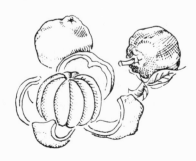

Cheese-Rice Salad

        1 teaspoon prepared mustard
        3 tablespoons cider vinegar
        2 tablespoons vegetable oil
        1 teaspoon salt
        ¼ teaspoon freshly ground black pepper
        ¼ teaspoon crushed oregano leaves
        2 green onions, minced
        ¼ cup sliced pimiento-stuffed olives or 1
             canned pimiento, minced
        ½ pound mozzarella cut into julienne strips
        ½ cup sharp Cheddar cheese cut into julienne
             strips
        2 cups cooked rice
        3 hard-cooked eggs, halved
          Paprika
          Chopped parsley

In mixing bowl, whip together the mustard, vinegar, oil, salt, pepper, oregano, and onions. Add olives, cheeses, and rice and toss lightly. Put in serving dish and garnish with egg halves. Sprinkle with paprika and parsley. Makes 4 to 6 servings.

Curried Rice and Crab-Meat Salad

        1 cup uncooked rice
        ½ cup chopped celery
        ½ cup chopped green pepper
        2 cans (6½ ounces each) crab meat, drained
             and flaked
        ¾ cup Mayonnaise*
        2 tablespoons lemon juice

½ teaspoon curry powder
 Salt
 Freshly ground pepper
3 pimientos, cut up

Cook rice according to package directions; drain and cool. Place in a bowl with celery, green pepper, and crab meat. Mix mayonnaise with lemon juice and curry powder and add to rice mixture. Season to taste with salt and pepper and fold in pimiento. Chill until serving time. Makes 6 servings.

Green Rice Salad

1 cup uncooked rice
¼ cup salad oil
¼ cup wine vinegar
3 tablespoons water
6 water chestnuts, chopped
½ cup minced parsley
¼ cup minced green onion
½ cup green pepper, chopped
½ cup chopped celery
1 cup cooked peas
½ cup Green-Goddess Dressing*

Cook rice according to package directions. While still hot, stir in salad oil, vinegar, and water. Cool. Add water chestnuts, parsley, onion, green pepper, celery, and peas and mix together. Toss thoroughly with dressing and chill. Makes 4 servings.

Tuna-Rice Salad

     1 cup uncooked rice
       Salt
     1 can (7 ounces) tuna, flaked
  1 ½ cups finely chopped celery
  1 ½ cups fine chopped carrots
     3 green onions, chopped
    ¼ cup chopped sweet pickle
    ¾ cup Mayonnaise*
    ¼ cup vinegar
     1 teaspoon dried thyme
    ¼ teaspoon freshly ground pepper
    ½ cup chopped parsley
       Boston lettuce leaves

Cook rice with salt according to package directions. Cool and mix with tuna, celery, carrots, onions, and pickle. Blend mayonnaise with vinegar, thyme, pepper, and parsley. Combine with rice mixture and toss thoroughly. Place salad in a 2-quart mixing bowl and press down to mold it. Cover and chill. Turn out on a round serving plate lined with lettuce leaves. Makes 4 to 6 servings.

Potato Salad

     2 scallions, sliced thin
     2 tablespoons minced parsley
     6 tablespoons oil
     4 tablespoons white-wine vinegar
    ½ teaspoon salt
    ⅛ teaspoon freshly ground pepper
     1 pound warm cooked small new potatoes,
         peeled and sliced ¼-inch thick

In a large bowl mix the scallions, parsley, oil, vinegar, salt, and pepper. Add potatoes; toss gently to coat well. Let stand for at least one hour. Serve at room temperature. Makes 4 servings.

Potato-Beet Salad with Deviled Ham

    6 medium potatoes, cooked, peeled, and diced
    1 can (1 pound) diced beets, drained
    4 medium carrots, peeled and diced
    1 medium onion, chopped
    1 cup Mayonnaise*
    1 can (2½ ounces) deviled ham
    1 teaspoon dry mustard
      Salt
      Freshly ground pepper

Place potatoes, beets, carrots, and onions in a large bowl. Mix well the mayonnaise, deviled ham, mustard, and salt and pepper to taste; fold gently into vegetable mixture. Cover and chill. Makes 6 servings.

Creamed Potato Salad

    1½ pounds potatoes, boiled, peeled, and diced
     1 cup diced celery
     2 tablespoons minced scallions or onions
     2 tablespoons wine vinegar
     ½ teaspoon salt
     ¼ teaspoon freshly ground pepper
     ½ cup dairy sour cream
     ½ cup heavy cream
       Lettuce

Place warm potatoes, celery, and scallions in a bowl. Combine the vinegar, salt, and pepper; pour over salad and toss. Chill well. Just before serving add combined sour cream and heavy cream; toss again gently. Adjust seasoning and serve in a lettuce-lined bowl. Makes 6 servings.

Curried Potato Salad

⅓ cup chicken broth
3 teaspoons curry powder
6 warm cooked large potatoes, peeled and
    cubed
6 scallions, minced
1 teaspoon salt
½ cup Mayonnaise*
2 tablespoons lemon juice
6 ribs celery, scraped and sliced thin
1 medium tart apple, diced
    Red and green apple slices

Heat the broth and blend in curry powder. Cook 1 or 2 minutes; cool slightly. In a bowl toss potatoes gently with scallions, curry-broth mixture, and salt; let stand until most of the broth is absorbed. Mix mayonnaise, lemon juice, celery, and tart apple and add to potato mixture. Toss gently. Cover and chill at least 2 hours. Garnish with apple slices. Makes 6 servings.

Potato and Green-Bean Salad

    1 pound warm cooked cut green beans
    5 warm cooked large potatoes, peeled and
        cubed
    2 scallions, minced
    ½ cup oil
    4 tablespoons white vinegar
    1 clove garlic, crushed
    1 small red onion, sliced thin
    ½ teaspoon oregano
    1 teaspoon dried thyme
    1 teaspoon salt
      Freshly ground pepper

Place beans, potatoes, and scallions in a bowl. Mix
thoroughly the oil, vinegar, garlic, red onion, oregano,
salt, and pepper and pour over the vegetables. Toss
gently. Serve warm or chilled. Makes 6 servings.

Herbed New-Potato Salad

    ½ cup Mayonnaise*
    ½ cup buttermilk or plain yogurt
    2 tablespoons snipped fresh dillweed or 2
        teaspoons dried
    2 tablespoons minced chives
    ½ teaspoon salt
    ⅛ teaspoon freshly ground pepper
 1½ pounds cooked small new potatoes (about
        12), quartered
      Watercress sprigs

In bowl mix well mayonnaise, buttermilk, dillweed, chives, salt, and pepper. Fold in potatoes. Cover and chill at least one hour. Spoon onto serving dish and garnish with watercress. Makes 4 servings.

Hot Potato Salad

        6 slices bacon, cut into ½-inch pieces
        2 tablespoons flour
     1 ½ teaspoons salt
        ⅛ teaspoon freshly ground pepper
        1 tablespoon sugar
        ⅓ cup cider vinegar
     1 ¼ cups water
        6 medium potatoes, cooked, peeled and sliced
        ½ cup thinly sliced celery
          Few thin slices red onion
          Chicory or escarole pieces (about 2 cups
             lightly packed)

Sauté bacon in large skillet until crisp. Remove bacon and pour off all but 3 tablespoons fat. Stir in flour, salt, pepper, and sugar. Add vinegar and water and bring to boil, stirring. Simmer 1 to 2 minutes. Add potatoes, celery, and onions, and heat gently. Transfer to a serving bowl and toss gently with chicory or escarole. Sprinkle with bacon. Makes 4 to 6 servings.

Spinach-Potato Salad

½ cup oil
¼ cup grated Parmesan cheese
4 tablespoons lemon juice
1 teaspoon salt
2 teaspoons Worcestershire sauce
¼ teaspoon freshly ground pepper
6 warm cooked large potatoes, peeled and
　　diced
4 cups shredded spinach
3 hard-cooked eggs, cut in quarters lengthwise

In large bowl mix the oil, cheese, lemon juice, salt, Worcestershire sauce, and pepper. Add potatoes; toss gently. Cover and chill. Gently mix in the spinach and garnish with eggs. Makes 6 servings.

SIX

The Slaw Salad

Coleslaw doesn't have to be just traditional shredded cabbage with a dressing. It can be made from a variety of vegetables from sweet juicy carrots to crunchy rutabagas; or for a change, use shredded apples or pears.

Slaws add crunchy texture to your menu, spark your meals with color, and are a good source of vitamins A and C. Here is a sampling of recipes with variations to give you a new slant on slaws. Why not create your own combinations?

Basic Coleslaw

> ½ cup Mayonnaise*
> ¼ cup French Dressing*
> ½ teaspoon sugar
> ¼ teaspoon freshly ground pepper
> 4 cups shredded cabbage

Combine the mayonnaise with the dressing, sugar, and pepper. Blend thoroughly. Toss the cabbage with the dressing, cover, and chill. Makes 6 servings.

VARIATIONS

I. Celery Coleslaw: Add 1 cup chopped celery and ½ cup chopped scallions to Basic Coleslaw.*

138

II. Tomato Coleslaw: Add 2 cups coarsely diced peeled tomatoes and 2 tablespoons chives to Basic Coleslaw.*

III. Apple Coleslaw: Add 2 cups diced unpeeled red apples, 1 tablespoon celery seed, and ½ cup chopped walnuts to Basic Coleslaw.*

IV. Cranberry Slaw: Add ¾ cup chopped cranberries, 1 tablespoon sugar, and 1 teaspoon grated orange rind to Basic Coleslaw.*

V. Orange Slaw: Add 1 cup mandarin or peeled orange sections and 2 tablespoons pimiento strips to Basic Coleslaw.*

VI. Pineapple Slaw: Add 1 cup drained pineapple tidbits and 2 tablespoons grated Cheddar cheese to Basic Coleslaw.*

Cream Coleslaw

     1 head cabbage, shredded (about 5 cups)
     ¾ cup heavy cream
     2 tablespoons white vinegar
     1 tablespoon sugar
     ¾ teaspoon salt
     ½ teaspoon freshly ground pepper
        Dash of hot-pepper sauce

Cut cabbage into 6 lengthwise wedges. Remove core, then slice cabbage crosswise as finely as possible. Place in a large bowl, pour on cream and sprinkle with vinegar, sugar, salt, pepper, and pepper sauce. Stir thoroughly with rubber spatula until cream begins to thicken slightly and little bubbles appear. Serve immediately. Makes 6 servings.

Hot Slaw

   1 head cabbage, shredded (about 5 cups)
      Boiling salted water
 ½ teaspoon salt
  2 teaspoons prepared mustard
  2 teaspoons sugar
 ¼ teaspoon white pepper
  2 tablespoons flour
  1 egg, beaten
 ¾ cup milk
  2 tablespoons butter
 ¼ cup cider vinegar
      Chopped parsley

Cook cabbage for two minutes in boiling salted water until crisp-tender. Drain well and keep warm. Combine and whip together salt, mustard, sugar, pepper, flour, and beaten egg; add milk and blend. Melt butter in double boiler. Stir in egg mixture. Slowly add vinegar, beating constantly, and cook 5 minutes, until sauce is thick and smooth. Pour over cabbage and mix well. Taste for seasoning. Spoon into heated serving dish and sprinkle with parsley. Makes 6 servings.

Marinated Coleslaw

   1 cup cider vinegar
  ½ cup sugar
  ¼ cup oil
  1 teaspoon each prepared mustard, celery
       seed, and salt
  ¼ teaspoon freshly ground pepper
  2 pounds green cabbage, 1 or 2 heads
       shredded (about 4 quarts)
  1 small onion, chopped
  1 jar (4 ounces) pimiento, chopped

Mix vinegar, sugar, oil, mustard, celery seed, salt, and pepper. Pour over cabbage, onion, and pimiento; toss to mix well. Cover and chill at least 24 hours. Salad keeps 3 to 4 days in refrigerator. Makes 12 servings.

Sour-Cream Slaw

  1 head cabbage, shredded (about 5 cups)
  1 cup dairy sour cream
  ⅓ cup sugar
  ½ teaspoon salt
  1 teaspoon prepared mustard
  2 tablespoons vinegar

Place the cabbage in a bowl. Combine sour cream, sugar, salt, mustard, and vinegar; blend thoroughly and pour over the cabbage. Mix well, cover, and chill. Makes 6 servings.

Beet Slaw

    ½ cup dairy sour cream
    2 tablespoons milk
    2 teaspoons horseradish
    ¼ teaspoon salt
    ⅛ teaspoon white pepper
    3 cups shredded beets (about 6 large beets)
    1 tart apple, cored and shredded
      Sliced blanched almonds
      Minced parsley

Blend together sour cream, milk, horseradish, salt, and pepper. Combine mixture with shredded beets and apple and mix thoroughly. Chill. Garnish with almonds and parsley. Makes 4 servings.

Broccoli and Red-Cabbage Salad

    ⅔ cup Mayonnaise*
    2 tablespoons sour cream
    2 tablespoons dill- or sweet-pickle juice
    2 green onions, minced
    ¼ teaspoon salt
    ⅛ teaspoon freshly ground pepper
    4 cups shredded red cabbage
    2 broccoli stalks, peeled and sliced thin (about
        2 cups)

With fork or whisk beat mayonnaise with sour cream and pickle juice until smooth; stir in onions, salt, and pepper. Spoon over cabbage and broccoli and toss to mix. Makes 4 to 6 servings.

Caraway Carrot Slaw

⅓ cup Mayonnaise*
⅓ cup buttermilk
½ teaspoon caraway seed
½ teaspoon salt
⅛ teaspoon freshly ground pepper
4 cups shredded carrots (1 pound)
½ cup chopped celery (2 small ribs)
3 medium-size green onions with tops, cut
    into ½-inch slices
Lettuce

In bowl mix well mayonnaise, buttermilk, caraway seed, salt, and pepper. Stir in carrots, celery, and onions. Cover and refrigerate at least one hour to blend flavors. Serve in lettuce-lined bowl. Makes 6 to 8 servings.

Carrot Slaw

1 pound coarsely shredded carrots (about 4 cups)
½ cup pitted dates, finely cut up
½ cup slivered almonds
½ cup dairy sour cream
¼ cup milk
1 tablespoon lemon juice
1 teaspoon sugar
¼ teaspoon salt
    Dash of white pepper
    Minced parsley

In a mixing bowl combine carrots, dates, and almonds. Blend sour cream, milk, lemon juice, sugar, salt, and pepper; pour over salad and toss thoroughly. Serve chilled garnished with parsley. Makes 6 servings.

Cauliflower Slaw

    3 cups coarsely shredded cauliflower, stalks
       included
    1 cup coarsely shredded large radishes
    1 tablespoon lemon juice
    ½ teaspoon dried or 2 teaspoons fresh
       chopped dill
    ½ teaspoon salt
    ⅛ teaspoon white pepper
    ¼ cup milk
    ⅓ cup Mayonnaise*

Place cauliflower and radishes in a bowl; sprinkle with lemon juice. Combine dill, salt, pepper, milk, and mayonnaise and blend well. Pour over vegetables and toss thoroughly. Chill. Makes 6 servings.

Cabbage-Grape Salad

    ½ cup Mayonnaise*
    2 tablespoons dairy sour cream
    1 teaspoon celery seed
    ½ teaspoon salt
    ¼ teaspoon white pepper
    5 cups shredded cabbage (1 pound)
    2 cups green or red grapes, halved and seeded
    ¾ cup chopped celery (2 large ribs)
      Chopped celery leaves for garnish (optional)

In large bowl mix well mayonnaise, sour cream, celery seed, salt, and pepper. Add cabbage, grapes, and celery. Toss lightly to mix well. If desired, serve in bowl lined with outer cabbage leaves. Garnish with celery leaves. Makes 6 to 8 servings.

Ham-Apple Slaw

    3 cups shredded cabbage
 1½ cups slivered ham
    2 medium apples, cored, unpeeled, and diced
   ⅓ cup Mayonnaise*
 2 to 3 tablespoons vinegar

Chill cabbage and ham in a bowl. Just before serving, add apples and toss with combined mayonnaise and vinegar. Makes 6 servings.

Celery-Apple Slaw

    4 cups celery, scraped and cut into very thin
         slivers
    2 tablespoons chopped scallions
    2 cups coarsely shredded apples
   ¼ cup chopped walnuts
   ½ cup Mayonnaise*
    2 tablespoons dairy sour cream
    1 tablespoon lemon juice
    1 teaspoon sugar

Place the celery, scallions, and apples in a bowl. Blend the mayonnaise with sour cream, lemon juice, and sugar. Toss with the salad. Serve chilled, preferably in a glass bowl. Makes 6 servings.

Ham and Cheese Slaw

   2 cups finely shredded red cabbage
   2 cups shredded green cabbage
   1 cup thinly sliced celery
   ½ cup Mayonnaise*
   ¼ cup dairy sour cream
   2 teaspoons prepared mustard
   ½ teaspoon salt
   ¼ teaspoon freshly ground pepper
   ¼ pound Swiss cheese, cut into julienne strips
   ¼ pound ham, cut into julienne strips

Combine cabbages and celery in a bowl. Blend together mayonnaise, sour cream, mustard, salt, and pepper; mix thoroughly with salad. Add cheese and ham and toss carefully. Chill. Makes 6 servings.

Lettuce Slaw

   1 large firm head iceberg lettuce
   ½ cup seedless grapes
   ½ cup shredded Cheddar cheese
   ⅓ cup Mustard French Dressing*
   1 tablespoon minced fresh or 1 teaspoon dried
      oregano

Cut the lettuce in quarters and then slice as thin as possible; cut the grapes in half if you wish. Combine the lettuce, grapes, and cheese and toss with the dressing. Sprinkle with oregano. Makes 4 servings.

Parsnip Slaw

 3 peeled and shredded parsnips (about 2½
   cups)
½ cup shredded sweet pickles
¼ cup chopped pimiento-stuffed olives
 2 tablespoons minced red onion
⅓ cup Mayonnaise*
 1 tablespoon lemon juice
¼ teaspoon salt
   Dash of white pepper
   Paprika

In a bowl place parsnips, pickles, olives, and onion. Add blended mayonnaise, lemon juice, salt, and pepper; toss thoroughly, sprinkle with paprika, and chill. Makes 4 servings.

Two-Pepper Slaw

 3 medium green peppers, seeded and
   quartered
 1 jar (7½ ounces) roasted sweet red peppers,
   drained
⅓ to ½ cup French Dressing*

Precook green peppers in lightly salted water for 3 minutes. Drain and cool. Slice both green and red peppers in ⅛ inch strips. Combine them with dressing, toss gently, and chill. Makes 4 servings.

Red Cabbage Slaw

      1 head red cabbage, shredded (about 4 cups)
    ½ cup diced green pepper
      1 cup coarsely chopped cranberries
    ½ cup Mayonnaise*
    ¼ cup orange juice
    ½ teaspoon salt
        Dash of white pepper
      2 tablespoons sugar

Cut the cabbage crosswise with a knife; core and slice about ⅛ inch thick. Combine with the peppers and cranberries in a bowl. Blend the mayonnaise with orange juice, salt, pepper, and sugar. Pour over the salad and toss. Makes 6 servings.

Rutabaga-Apple Slaw

      1 cup coarsely grated peeled rutabaga
      1 cup shredded cabbage
      1 cup diced unpeeled red apples
    ¼ cup raisins
    ¼ cup chopped peanuts
      1 tablespoon lemon juice
    ¼ cup Cooked Salad Dressing* or
          Mayonnaise*

Mix rutabaga, cabbage, apples, raisins, and peanuts in a bowl. Combine lemon juice and salad dressing; add to salad and toss well. Makes 4 servings.

Spinach Slaw

    1 pound young spinach, shredded (about 4 cups)
    ½ cup shredded sweet red peppers
    ⅓ cup Cooked Salad Dressing*
      Pinch nutmeg

Remove heavy stems from the spinach. Wash and dry the leaves and cut them into shreds. Mix the spinach and red peppers with the dressing and nutmeg. Toss thoroughly and serve at once. Makes 4 servings.

White Turnip Slaw

    6 medium turnips, peeled and shredded (about 3 cups)
    ½ cup slivered pitted black olives
    ¼ cup chopped red onion
    ⅓ cup Herb French Dressing*

Mix the turnips, olives, and onion in a serving bowl. Pour the dressing over the salad and toss. Cover and chill. Makes 4 servings.

Zucchini Slaw

    4 medium zucchini, unpeeled and shredded
    1 large pimiento, chopped
    2 tablespoons minced chives
    3 tablespoons chopped parsley
    ⅓ cup Italian Dressing*

Combine the zucchini, pimiento, chives, and parsley in a salad bowl and toss with the dressing. Serve chilled in lettuce cups. Makes 4 to 6 servings.

SEVEN

The Sprout Salad

modern salads at their best

Sprouts are springing up all over! Crunchy and delicious, low in calories, high in fiber, and rich in vitamins and minerals, they are a treat for salad-lovers and an inspiration to salad-chefs.

Best of all, they are always in season, inexpensive, available in supermarkets, and easy to grow at home. With little effort you and your family can become sprout farmers and watch them grow in your own kitchen.

The easiest ones to grow are mung bean sprouts. Place one-quarter cup of mung bean seeds in a bowl. Cover the seeds with warm water and leave overnight—they will swell. Rinse them in a strainer under cold running water and drain, but do not dry them. Put the seeds in a quart jar placed on its side, or any nonmetal flat-bottom dish, and cover with wet cheesecloth held in place with a rubber band. Keep them in a dimly lit warm place—68° F to 80° F. Rinse and drain the seeds twice a day, always returning them to their container and replacing the wet cheesecloth cover. After 3 to 4 days the seeds will have sprouted. If you want longer "tails" on your sprouts, wait another day. Yield: one and a half cups sprouts.

Avocado-Alfalfa Sprout Salad

3 cups alfalfa sprouts
2 avocados, peeled and diced
2 tablespoons lemon juice
1 pimiento, cut in strips
18 pitted black olives
¼ cup olive oil
2 tablespoons vinegar
1 clove garlic, crushed
1 teaspoon salt
¼ teaspoon freshly ground pepper

Put the sprouts into a glass bowl and separate with your fingers. Add the avocado and sprinkle with lemon juice. Arrange pimiento strips and olives over salad. Combine oil, vinegar, garlic, salt, and pepper and mix well. Pour over the salad and toss gently. Makes 6 servings.

Bean-Sprout Bacon Salad

4 slices bacon
⅓ cup wine vinegar
1 clove garlic, crushed
½ teaspoon Worcestershire sauce
⅛ teaspoon dry mustard
¾ teaspoon salt
⅛ teaspoon freshly ground pepper
1 pound fresh mung bean sprouts or 1 can (16 ounces), drained
2 tablespoons chopped scallions
3 tablespoons minced green pepper
2 tablespoons minced pimiento

Fry the bacon until crisp, crumble, and set aside. Mix the vinegar with ⅓ cup bacon drippings. Add garlic, Worcestershire sauce, mustard, salt, and pepper. Heat this mixture. Place bean sprouts in boiling water for one minute to wilt them; drain. Put sprouts in a salad bowl with the scallions, green pepper, and pimiento. Top with the hot dressing. Marinate at room temperature for an hour. Add the crumbled bacon and toss. Makes 4 servings.

Mung-Bean-Sprout, Celery, and Apple Salad

      1 can (1 pound) drained, or 1 pound fresh
            mung bean sprouts
      1 cup chopped celery
      1 medium red apple, unpeeled and chopped
      2 green onions, minced
      ½ cup well-seasoned French* or Lemon
            French Dressing*

If using fresh bean sprouts place them in a collander, pour boiling water over them, and drain. If using canned sprouts refresh them in ice water for 2 minutes, then drain. Combine sprouts, celery, apple, and onions in a salad bowl. Add dressing, toss lightly, and serve at once. Makes 4 to 6 servings.

Bean-Sprout and Chicken Salad

      2 cups cooked chicken, cut into julienne strips
      2 cups fresh mung bean sprouts (about ¾
            pound) or 1 can (16 ounces), drained

½ cup sliced water chestnuts (about ½ an
     8-ounce can)
½ cup chopped green pepper
2 green onions with tops, minced
¼ cup oil
3 tablespoons soy sauce
2 tablespoons vinegar
2 teaspoons grated ginger
1 teaspoon sugar
  Salt
  Freshly ground pepper
6 lettuce cups

Combine chicken, bean sprouts, water chestnuts, green pepper, and onions in a bowl. Mix oil, soy sauce, vinegar, ginger, sugar, salt and pepper to taste, and pour over salad; toss lightly. Spoon into lettuce cups. Makes 6 servings.

Green Bean and Sprout Salad

4 cups french-cut green beans
1 pound fresh mung bean sprouts or 1 can (1
     pound) drained
½ cup minced scallions
1 cup thinly sliced celery
2 pimientos, minced
½ cup salad oil
¼ cup cider vinegar
1 teaspoon salt
¼ teaspoon freshly ground black pepper
½ teaspoon sugar
  Cherry tomatoes

Cook beans until crisp-tender, drain, and cool. Place fresh bean sprouts in boiling water for 1 minute, rinse, and drain. If using canned sprouts, rinse in ice water and drain. In a mixing bowl combine green beans, bean sprouts, scallions, celery, and pimientos. Blend together oil, vinegar, salt, pepper, and sugar and pour over the vegetables. Toss and chill. Garnish with cherry tomatoes. Makes 8 servings.

Mushroom and Bean-Sprout Salad

    2 cups fresh mung bean sprouts or 1 can
          (1 pound), drained
    1 pound mushrooms, sliced thin
    ¼ cup olive oil
    2 tablespoons wine vinegar
    1 teaspoon prepared mustard
    1 clove garlic, crushed
    ¼ cup chopped parsley
    ⅛ teaspoon oregano
    ½ teaspoon basil
    1 teaspoon salt
    ¼ teaspoon freshly ground pepper

Blanch fresh sprouts in boiling water for 1 minute, drain. Refresh canned sprouts in ice water and drain. Place the mushrooms and sprouts in a serving bowl. Combine oil, vinegar, mustard, garlic, parsley, oregano, basil, salt, and pepper; mix thoroughly. Pour over the salad and toss. Makes 6 servings.

Oranges and Bean Sprouts with Water Chestnuts

        3 large oranges, peeled and sectioned
        1 pound fresh or 1 can (1 pound) mung bean
             sprouts, drained
        1 can (8 ounces) water chestnuts, sliced thin
        2 teaspoons soy sauce
        1 cup Honey Lime Dressing*
           Lettuce leaves

If using canned sprouts, rinse in ice water and drain them. If using fresh sprouts, blanch them for 1 minute in boiling water, rinse, and drain. Combine the oranges with the bean sprouts. Add ⅔ of the water chestnuts. Blend soy sauce with the dressing. Pour over the salad and toss to moisten evenly. Serve on crisp lettuce leaves and garnish with remaining water chestnuts. Makes 6 servings.

Oriental Sprout Salad

        1 small head lettuce, broken into bite-size pieces
        1 cucumber, sliced thin
     1½ cups fresh mung bean sprouts, blanched
        1 cup sliced mushrooms
        3 medium tomatoes, quartered
        2 teaspoons soy sauce
       ½ cup French Dressing*

Combine the lettuce, cucumber, sprouts, and mushrooms in a shallow salad bowl. Top with the tomato wedges. Add soy sauce to the dressing, pour over the salad, and toss gently. Makes 4 servings.

Spinach-Sprout Salad

    3 cups (about ¾ pound) fresh mung bean
        sprouts or 1 can (1 pound) bean sprouts, drained
    4 cups torn spinach leaves
    ½ cup salad oil
    ¼ cup cider vinegar
    3 tablespoons chili sauce
    ½ teaspoon salt
      Freshly ground pepper
    2 hard-cooked eggs, quartered

Place fresh sprouts in a collander; pour boiling water over them; rinse and drain. If using canned sprouts rinse in ice water and drain. Combine spinach and sprouts in a bowl. Mix oil, vinegar, chili sauce, salt, and pepper; toss with the salad and garnish with egg quarters. Makes 6 servings.

Tomato Salad with Alfalfa Sprouts

    4 large ripe tomatoes, peeled and sliced
    2 teaspoons sugar
 1½ cups alfalfa sprouts
    4 scallions, chopped
    2 tablespoons minced parsley
    1 teaspoon salt
    ½ teaspoon freshly ground pepper
    1 teaspoon lemon juice
    ¼ cup olive oil

Sprinkle sugar on tomato slices. Place half the tomatoes on a platter. Cover with the sprouts and half the scallions. Combine parsley, salt, pepper, lemon juice, and oil.

Dribble some of the dressing over the sprouts. Arrange remaining tomatoes over the sprouts. Sprinkle with remaining scallions, parsley and dressing. Makes 6 servings.

Waldorf-Sprout Salad

    2 cups fresh or 1 can (1 pound), drained mung
        bean sprouts
    2 apples, unpeeled and diced
    1 cup chopped celery
    ½ cup chopped walnuts
    1 cup Mayonnaise*
    3 tablespoons Fresh Dressing,* or light cream

Pour boiling water over fresh sprouts; drain. Rinse canned sprouts in ice water and drain. Combine with the apples, celery, and nuts. Thin ½ cup mayonnaise with fresh dressing or cream. Pour over the salad and toss. Add enough mayonnaise to make the salad moist, but not too wet. Makes 6 servings.

Watercress Salad with Alfalfa Sprouts

    2 bunches watercress
 1½ cups alfalfa sprouts
    1 cup chickpeas, drained
   ¼ cup minced red onion
    1 tablespoon capers
    ½ cup Italian Dressing*
    1 cup garlic croutons

Wash the watercress and remove heavy stems. Put the cress in a bowl with the sprouts and chickpeas and mix well. Combine the onion and capers with the dressing; mix, and pour over the salad. Toss. Sprinkle with croutons. Makes 6 servings.

Zucchini, Alfalfa Sprout, and Sesame Salad

    2 cups shredded unpeeled zucchini
    1 cup shredded carrots
    2 cups alfalfa sprouts
    2 tablespoons chopped scallions
    6 tablespoons salad oil
    2 tablespoons lemon juice
    2 tablespoons vinegar
    ½ teaspoon dried basil
    1 teaspoon salt
    ¼ teaspoon freshly ground pepper
    4 tablespoons sesame seeds, toasted

Place zucchini, carrots, sprouts, and scallions in a salad bowl and mix together. Combine the oil, lemon juice, vinegar, basil, salt, and pepper; blend well. Pour over the zucchini-sprouts mixture and toss. Add the sesame seeds and toss again. Makes 6 servings.

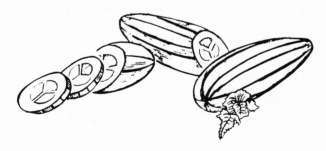

EIGHT

The Basic Vegetable Salad
raw vegetables

Chopped, grated, sliced, or shredded, raw vegetables—flavorful, crisp, and nutritious—reach their zenith in salads. If you're lucky enough to have a garden, your salads will be the epitome of healthy freshness and flavor. If you must buy them, choose the freshest legumes to serve raw—select what is in peak season as well as what is at its peak in season!

Since they require no cooking, raw vegetable salads conserve precious energy. They are good for the teeth and gums and will give you an outer shine and an inner glow.

Winter Buffet Salad and Trio of Dressings

    3 cups shredded red cabbage
    2 cups shredded carrots (2 large)
    2 cups scraped, thinly sliced celery (about 4)
    2 cups thinly sliced white turnips (about 4 small)
    2 cups thinly sliced cauliflowerettes
    2 cups thinly sliced broccoli stalks (about 2
            stalks, peeled)
    1 cup thinly sliced radishes
    3 or 4 broccoli flowerettes for decoration
    1 cup Green French Dressing*
    1 cup Russian Dressing*
    1 cup Pimiento Vinaigrette Dressing*

Arrange cabbage, carrots, celery, turnips, cauliflowerettes, broccoli stalks, and radishes in separate mounds on serving platter. Decorate platter with broccoli flowerettes. Place each dressing in a small bowl and serve with salad. Makes 10 to 12 servings. NOTE: Recipe can be halved or restricted to desired vegetables.

Caesar Salad

1 coddled egg
8 cups torn romaine lettuce
3 tablespoons grated Parmesan cheese
Salt
Freshly ground pepper
3 tablespoons lemon juice
½ cup plus 1 tablespoon salad oil
¼ teaspoon Worcestershire sauce
Croutons

Cook egg in boiling water for 1 minute; remove and set aside. Arrange well-chilled romaine leaves in a large bowl; sprinkle with Parmesan cheese, salt, and pepper. Break egg over salad and toss until leaves are well coated. Combine lemon juice, oil, and Worcestershire sauce; add to romaine and toss. Add croutons and serve at once. Makes 6 servings.

Croutons: Cut 6 to 8 slices of bread into ½-inch squares, using firm-type French or Italian bread with the crust removed. In bowl, mash 1 clove garlic with fork. Add ¼ to ½ teaspoon salt to garlic and mix. Add bread cubes, sprinkle with 2 to 3 tablespoons salad oil, and toss until well coated. Bake in shallow pan or on baking sheet in preheated 350°F oven 12 to 15 minutes, or until golden. Drain on absorbent paper.

Raw Cauliflower-Olive Salad

    1 large head cauliflower, about 3 to 4 cups
          flowerettes
    1 pound large ripe olives, pitted and sliced
    3 scallions, chopped fine
       Grated rind of 1 lemon
    ½ cup Lemon French Dressing*
       Salad greens

Break the cauliflower into small flowerettes. Combine the cauliflower, olives, scallions, and grated lemon rind. Toss thoroughly with the dressing. Taste for seasoning; cover and chill. Serve on a platter lined with greens. Makes 6 servings.

Cauliflower-Romaine Salad

    ¼ cup oil
    2 tablespoons chili sauce
    2 tablespoons lemon juice or wine vinegar
    1 tablespoon water
    2 teaspoons horseradish (optional)
    ¼ teaspoon salt
    ⅛ teaspoon freshly ground pepper
    2 cups thinly sliced cauliflowerettes
    3 cups packed romaine, cut crosswise in
          ¼-inch shreds

Mix oil, chili sauce, lemon juice, water, horseradish, salt, and pepper. Pour over cauliflowerettes and romaine, toss lightly, and serve at once. Makes 4 servings.

Celery Salad

    1 bunch celery, scraped and slivered (about 4
         cups)
    2 carrots, scraped and slivered
    1 tablespoon grated ginger root
    2 tablespoons soy sauce
    ½ cup Italian Dressing*

Soak celery and carrots in enough ice water to cover for ½
hour, then drain. Sprinkle with ginger, cover, and refrigerate until ready to serve. Just before serving, toss vegetables with a mixture of soy sauce and dressing. Makes
6 servings.

Citrus Winter Salad

    ¼ cup oil
    ¼ cup lemon juice
    2 teaspoons sugar
      Salt
      Freshly ground pepper
    6 cups torn romaine
    1 cup orange sections (2 medium)
    1 cup grapefruit sections (1 large)
    ⅓ cup small green onions with tops, cut into
         1-inch slices

In salad bowl mix well oil, lemon juice, sugar, salt, and
pepper to taste. Add romaine, orange and grapefruit
sections, and green onions. Toss lightly to coat, arranging
grapefruit and oranges in pinwheel pattern in center of
salad. Serve at once. Makes 4 to 6 servings.

Cucumber-Yogurt Salad

      2 cups plain yogurt
      1 clove garlic, minced
      ½ teaspoon salt
      2 teaspoons sugar
      2 tablespoons minced coriander or parsley
      3 medium cucumbers, peeled, seeded, and
            thinly sliced

Combine the yogurt, garlic, salt, sugar, and coriander or parsley and mix well. Adjust seasoning. Stir in the cucumbers and chill. Makes 6 servings.

Fennel, Yogurt, and Walnut Salad

      1½ pounds fennel bulbs
      1 cup plain yogurt
      2 tablespoons lemon juice
      1 teaspoon salt
      ¼ teaspoon freshly ground pepper
      1 tablespoon minced fresh or 1 teaspoon dry
            thyme or tarragon
      ¼ cup chopped walnuts
        Shredded lettuce

Trim the base of the fennel bulbs, remove any tough outer pieces, and slice the bulbs crosswise into thin slices. Reserve some of the feathery greens for garnish. Combine the yogurt, lemon juice, salt, pepper, and thyme or tarragon. Place the fennel and walnuts in a serving bowl, pour the dressing over them, toss, and chill. Just before serving, garnish with the fennel leaves and serve on the shredded lettuce. Makes 6 servings.

Lettuce and Crouton Salad

  1 medium head Boston lettuce
  1 bunch red leaf lettuce
  ½ cup Italian Dressing*
  1 onion, minced
  2 hard-cooked eggs, chopped fine
  ½ cup garlic croutons

Wash and dry the lettuces and tear into bite-size pieces. Fill a salad bowl with the greens. Pour the dressing over the salad and toss. Sprinkle with minced onion and chopped eggs. Top with croutons and toss gently. Makes 6 servings.

Tossed Mushroom Salad

  ½ pound fresh thinly sliced mushrooms or 1
      can (6 to 8 ounces) sliced mushrooms,
      drained
  1 cup scraped, diced celery
  ½ cup sliced green onions
  ¼ cup tomato juice
  2 tablespoons chopped parsley
  1 tablespoon lemon juice
1¼ teaspoons salt
  ⅛ teaspoon freshly ground pepper

Put mushrooms in large bowl and add celery and green onions. In small bowl mix tomato juice, parsley, lemon juice, salt, and pepper. Pour over mushroom mixture, cover, and refrigerate. Makes 4 servings.

Mushroom Soy Salad

1 pound mushrooms, wiped and sliced very
   thin
2 tablespoons olive oil
2 tablespoons Worcestershire sauce
2 tablespoons soy sauce
½ teaspoon salt
¼ teaspoon freshly ground pepper
½ clove garlic, crushed (optional)

Place the mushrooms in a bowl. Combine the oil, Worcestershire sauce, soy sauce, salt, pepper, and garlic and mix well. Pour over the mushrooms and toss gently. Chill for at least an hour. Makes 4 servings.

Mushroom-Cress Salad

⅓ cup oil
2 tablespoons tarragon, white-wine, or white
   vinegar
¼ teaspoon salt
   Freshly ground pepper to taste
6 cups watercress leaves (about 3 bunches)
½ pound mushrooms, sliced thin

In salad bowl mix well oil, vinegar, salt, and pepper. Add watercress and mushrooms. Toss lightly to coat. If desired, stand some mushroom slices on end around rim of bowl to create scalloped garnish. Serve at once. Makes 6 to 8 servings.

Green Pepper and Tomato Salad

    3 green peppers
    3 large tomatoes, peeled
    ½ teaspoon salt
    ½ teaspoon freshly ground pepper
    ½ teaspoon sugar
    2 tablespoons salad oil
    1 can (4 ounces) anchovy fillets

Scorch the peppers, holding them on a long-handled fork over a gas flame until black. (Hold over electric heat until blistered.) Rub the skins off under cold running water. Seed and slice them. Alternate slices of pepper and tomato on a serving plate. Sprinkle with salt, pepper, and sugar. Combine the salad oil with oil from the anchovies and dribble the mixture over the salad. Top with anchovy fillets arranged in criss cross fashion over the vegetables. Makes 6 servings.

Tomatoes Stuffed with Avocado

    6 tomatoes
    1 large avocado, peeled and diced
    2 teaspoons lemon juice
    ½ cup Mayonnaise*
    1 teaspoon prepared mustard
    ½ teaspoon sugar
    ½ teaspoon salt
    ½ teaspoon freshly ground pepper
    1 teaspoon sugar
    2 tablespoons minced parsley or basil
      Lettuce or watercress

Cut tops from the tomatoes and spoon out the flesh. Drain and chop the tomato flesh. Place tomatoes upside down to drain. Sprinkle the diced avocado with half the lemon juice. Combine the mayonnaise with the mustard, sugar, salt, pepper, remaining lemon juice, tomato flesh, and minced parsley or basil. Gently mix in the avocado and fill the tomatoes. Serve on crisp lettuce or garnish with watercress. Makes 6 servings.

Zucchini-Yogurt Salad

      6 small zucchini, scrubbed and thinly sliced
           (about 6 cups)
      2 tablespoons chopped parsley
      3 tablespoons lemon juice
      2 tablespoons salad oil
      ½ teaspoon salt
        Freshly ground pepper to taste
      1 clove garlic, scored
      ½ cup plain yogurt
      3 cups shredded salad greens
      ⅓ cup finely chopped radishes
      ⅓ cup sliced pitted black olives

Combine zucchini, parsley, lemon juice, oil, salt, pepper, and garlic; cover and chill one hour. Discard garlic. Combine zucchini mixture and yogurt and serve mound on a bed of greens. Top with radishes and olives. Makes 6 servings.

NINE

Cooked Vegetables in Salads

Like jogging and yoga, cooked vegetables have come into their own and salads offer versatile time-saving ways to serve them. The next time you cook lentils, think "salad" instead of soup. Whether you serve delicate leeks with a vinaigrette sauce or a medley of marinated vegetables, remember what we've learned from the Chinese—cook vegetables only until crisp-tender. This method preserves vitamins and produces texture and flavor at its best.

Curried Vegetable Salad

  1 can (12 ounces) Mexican-style corn, drained
  1 cup cooked cut green beans
  1 cup cooked green lima beans
  2 hard-cooked eggs, chopped
  ¼ cup Mayonnaise*
  ¼ cup dairy sour cream
  2 tablespoons minced onion
  ½ teaspoon curry powder
  1 teaspoon prepared mustard
    Dash of Worcestershire and hot pepper
      sauce
    Lettuce cups
    Paprika

Place corn, green beans, lima beans and eggs in bowl. Blend mayonnaise, sour cream, onion, curry, mustard, Worcestershire, and hot pepper sauce and add to mixture. Toss well and chill. Serve in lettuce cups and sprinkle with paprika. Makes 6 servings.

Marinated Vegetable Salad

    1 small head cauliflower, cut into flowerettes
    2 stalks celery, scraped and sliced thin
    1 green pepper, cut into slivers
    2 carrots, scraped and sliced
    6 small white onions, sliced
    ½ cup wine vinegar
    ¼ cup oil, part olive
    1 teaspoon salt
    ¼ teaspoon freshly ground pepper
    2 teaspoons sugar
    1 teaspoon oregano
    1 teaspoon thyme
    ½ cup water

Place cauliflower, celery, green pepper, carrots, and onions in a pot. Combine vinegar, oil, salt, pepper, sugar, herbs, and water and pour over vegetables. Bring to a boil; cover and simmer 3 minutes. Cool and refrigerate overnight. Makes 6 servings.

Mixed Vegetable Salad

    1 cup cooked cut green beans
    1 cup cooked diced carrots
    1 cup cooked green peas
    1 cup diced cooked or canned beets, drained
    1 cup diced cooked potato
    3 green onions, sliced thin
    ⅓ cup well-seasoned French dressing*
      Mayonnaise*
      Salt
      Freshly ground pepper
      Salad greens

Combine beans, carrots, peas, beets, potato, green onions, and dressing. Toss lightly to mix and marinate one hour or longer. Just before serving, add enough mayonnaise to bind vegetables. Season with salt and pepper. Spoon into salad bowl lined with greens. Makes 6 servings.

NOTE: Any favorite cooked vegetables can be used.

Hot Kidney-Bean Salad

    4 slices bacon, cut crosswise into ½-inch
        pieces
    2 tablespoons chopped onion
    1 teaspoon flour
    3 tablespoons vinegar
    1 tablespoon sugar
    1 teaspoon salt
    ⅛ teaspoon freshly ground pepper
    1 can (1 pound) kidney beans, drained
    ½ cup chopped celery
    2 tablespoons chopped parsley

Sauté bacon in skillet until crisp. Remove; pour off all but 3 tablespoons fat. Add onion and sauté until tender. Stir in flour, vinegar, sugar, salt, and pepper. Add beans and simmer until heated. Add celery and parsley and mix gently. Sprinkle with crisp bacon. Makes 3 or 4 servings.

Two-Bean Salad

  ½ cup dairy sour cream
   2 tablespoons wine vinegar
   3 tablespoons prepared mustard
  ¼ teaspoon hot pepper sauce
  ½ teaspoon salt
   1 package (10 ounces) frozen cut, cooked, and
       drained, or 2 cups cooked fresh green
       beans
   1 can (1 pound) red kidney beans, drained
   2 tablespoons finely chopped green pepper
     Lettuce

Blend sour cream with vinegar, mustard, hot pepper sauce, and salt. Combine green beans, kidney beans, and green pepper in a bowl; stir in sour-cream mixture. Let stand at least an hour to blend flavors. Serve on crisp lettuce. Makes 6 servings.

Sweet-Sour Bean Salad

  1 cup cooked white kidney beans, drained
  1 can (1 pound) red kidney beans, drained
  1 can (20 ounces) chickpeas, drained
  2 green onions, thinly sliced
  ½ cup sliced celery
  ½ green pepper, thinly sliced (or part red
      pepper or pimiento)
  ⅓ cup salad oil
  ½ cup vinegar
  3 tablespoons sugar
  ½ teaspoon salt
  ⅛ teaspoon freshly ground pepper
    Boston lettuce

Put white and red kidney beans, chickpeas, onions, celery, and green pepper in large bowl. Combine oil, vinegar, sugar, salt, and pepper; pour over vegetables and mix gently. Chill several hours or overnight. Serve on Boston lettuce. Makes 6 to 8 servings.

Creamy Beet Salad

  6 large cooked beets, quartered and sliced
  1 large sweet onion, quartered and sliced thin
  ½ cup Mayonnaise*
  2 tablespoons vinegar
  2 tablespoons dairy sour cream
  1 teaspoon dried chervil
    Salt
    Freshly ground pepper

Put the beets and onions in a bowl. Combine the mayonnaise, vinegar, sour cream, and chervil. Season to taste with salt and pepper. Pour over the salad, toss gently, and chill. Makes 4 to 6 servings.

Cauliflower-Anchovy Salad

  1 large head cauliflower
  1 tablespoon lemon juice
  1 tablespoon vinegar
  ½ cup olive oil
  6 anchovy fillets, cut up
  ¼ teaspoon freshly ground pepper

Remove core and cook the whole cauliflower in boiling salted water until crisp-tender, about 10 minutes. Drain and chill. Combine the lemon juice, vinegar, oil, anchovies, and pepper; mix thoroughly. Separate the cauliflower into flowerettes and put in a salad bowl. Pour the dressing over the salad and toss gently. Serve at once. Makes 6 servings.

Celery Victor

  6 small whole celery hearts
  1½ to 2 cups chicken or beef broth
    Watercress
  1¼ cups Vinaigrette* or French Dressing*
    Minced parsley

Wash celery hearts and trim off top leaves. Simmer gently in broth until tender. Remove carefully, drain, and chill. Serve on six individual salad plates. Spoon 3 tablespoons dressing over each heart and sprinkle with parsley. Makes 6 servings.
NOTE: If celery hearts are large use 3 and cut them lengthwise, serving half to each person.

Chickpea and Red-Onion Salad

> 2 cans (1 pound each) chickpeas, drained
> 2 red onions, sliced thin
> ⅓ cup chopped Italian parsley
> ¾ cup Italian Dressing*
>   Tomato wedges
> ½ pound Greek olives
>   Salad greens

Combine chickpeas, onions, parsley, and dressing in a salad bowl and marinate 30 minutes or longer in refrigerator. Serve on a platter lined with greens. Surround with tomato wedges and olives. Makes 6 servings.

Leek Salad

> 6 large leeks
>   Simmering salted water
> ½ teaspoon prepared mustard
> 2 tablespoons minced parsley
> 1 hard-cooked egg, grated
> ¾ cup French Dressing*

Trim the roots of the leeks. Pull off any tough outside leaves and cut the tops, leaving about 2 or 3 inches of green. Slice the leeks in half lengthwise and wash under cold running water to remove sand. Simmer in enough salted water to cover until tender, about 15 minutes. Remove carefully; drain and chill. Arrange 2 halves on each of 6 salad plates. Add mustard, parsley, and grated egg to the dressing and mix thoroughly. Pour some dressing over each salad and serve. Makes 6 servings.

Lentil Salad

½ pound dried quick-cooking lentils
3 cups water
2 teaspoons salt
½ cup chopped parsley
½ cup minced scallions
⅓ cup French Dressing*
1 clove garlic, minced
Salt
Freshly ground pepper
Salad greens

In large saucepan, cover washed lentils with the water and the salt. Bring slowly to boil and simmer 30 minutes, or until tender. Drain and chill. In a mixing bowl combine lentils with parsley, scallions, and dressing blended with garlic. Mix thoroughly. Season to taste with salt and pepper and serve on crisp greens. Makes 4 servings.

Hearts of Palm Salad

1 can (13 ounces) hearts of palm, drained and
    chilled
Salad greens or watercress
½ cup French Dressing*
1 tablespoon chopped pimiento
1 tablespoon minced parsley

Leave the thin palms whole and split the thick ones lengthwise. Cut them crosswise into 2-inch pieces and arrange them on a watercress-lined serving dish. Pour the dressing over the salad and sprinkle with pimiento and parsley. Toss lightly. Makes 4 servings.

TEN

Molded Salads

A good way to initiate novice chefs, young and old alike, is to have them prepare a molded salad, mousse, or aspic. The results, delicious and spectacular to see, will encourage further ventures in the kitchen.

Molded salads lend themselves to any part of a meal. Serve shimmering vegetable aspic as an appetizer or heap chilled shrimp vinaigrette into the center of an avocado ring mold for a lucious main course. Fruit molds are among the most delectible desserts (recipes for these salads are in Chapter Eleven, The Dessert Salad).

To ensure proper setting make molded salads a day before you serve them. To facilitate unmolding, wet a mold before filling it. To unmold a salad, run the tip of a thin sharp knife around the edge of the mold. Dip the mold in hot water almost up to its brim, until the contents begin to loosen—less than a minute. Some cooks prefer to wrap a hot, wet towel around the mold. Place a cold platter, large enough to hold the salad and its garnishes, over the mold and turn it upside down. Tap the mold gently and remove it.

Creamy Avocado Mold

    3 avocados
    ¼ cup lemon juice
    1 tablespoon minced parsley
    1 tablespoon minced scallions
    1 clove garlic, crushed
    1 teaspoon salt
    2 packages (3 ounces each) cream cheese,
        softened
    1 cup light cream
 1 ½ envelopes unflavored gelatin
    ¼ cup cold water
    ¼ cup boiling water
      Watercress

Peel and mash the avocados and sprinkle at once with
lemon juice. Add the parsley, scallions, garlic, and salt.
Smooth the cream cheese with the cream. Add the avocado mixture and blend well. Soften the gelatin in cold
water. Add boiling water, then heat and stir to dissolve
the gelatin. Cool slightly and add to the avocado-cheese
mixture. Blend thoroughly. Spoon into a wet 6-cup mold
and chill until set. Unmold and garnish with watercress.
Makes 6 servings.

Beet-Horseradish Gelatin Salad

1 jar (16 ounces) whole beets
2 envelopes unflavored gelatin
1 cup cold water
¼ cup vinegar
2 tablespoons prepared horseradish
1 teaspoon lemon juice
½ teaspoon salt
½ cup chopped celery
Crisp greens
Horseradish Dressing*

Drain beets (reserve juice), dice into ½-inch cubes, and set aside. Sprinkle gelatin over cold water in small saucepan. Cook and stir over low heat until gelatin dissolves, about 3 minutes. Remove from heat and stir in vinegar, horseradish, lemon juice, and salt. Add enough water to reserved beet juice to make 2¼ cups and stir into gelatin mixture. Chill until thickened and very syrupy. Fold in beets and celery. Turn into a wet 6-cup mold and chill until firm. Unmold on greens and serve with horseradish dressing. Makes 4 to 6 servings.

Blue-Cheese Molded Salad

2 envelopes unflavored gelatin
1 cup cold water
4 tablespoons white wine
2 teaspoons lemon juice
2 teaspoons Worcestershire sauce
6 ounces blue cheese
6 ounces cream cheese
1 cup heavy cream, whipped
Salad greens

Soften the gelatin in ½ cup cold water. Boil remaining water, add to gelatin, and stir to dissolve. Mix in wine, lemon juice, and Worcestershire sauce. Chill until syrupy. Blend the cheeses together until creamy, mix well with the gelatin, and fold in the whipped cream. Spoon into a wet 4-cup mold and chill until firm. Unmold on greens and surround with crisp raw vegetables, or serve as a dessert with a bowl of fresh, sweetened berries. Makes 4 to 6 servings.

Cauliflower-Radish Mold

    2 envelopes unflavored gelatin
    1 cup cold water
    1 envelope instant vegetable broth
    ¼ cup sugar
    ½ teaspoon salt
 1 ½ cups ice water
    ¼ cup lemon juice
    1 cup thinly sliced cauliflower
      Radishes
    2 tablespoons chopped green onion
      Preferred salad dressing

Sprinkle gelatin over cold water in small saucepan. Cook and stir over low heat until gelatin dissolves, about 3 minutes. Revove from heat and stir in powdered broth, sugar, and salt until dissolved. Add ice water and lemon juice. Chill until thickened and very syrupy. Fold in cauliflower, ¼ cup sliced radishes, and the green onion. Turn into a wet 1-quart ring mold and chill until firm. Unmold on serving plate, fill center with whole radishes, if desired, and serve with salad dressing. Makes 4 to 6 servings.

Curried Corn Salad

½ cup chicken broth
1 package (10 ounces) frozen corn
1 teaspoon curry powder
1 tablespoon lemon juice
1 envelope plus 1 teaspoon unflavored gelatin
½ cup cold water
2 tablespoons minced green onion
2 pimientos, well drained and chopped
Lemon Mayonnaise*
Chutney (optional)

In a saucepan, heat chicken broth. Bring to boil, add corn, and cook, covered, until tender. Drain well, reserving broth, and chill corn. To reserved broth, add curry powder and lemon juice. Soften gelatin in ½ cup cold water. Place over low heat, stirring until gelatin dissolves. Add to broth with enough water to make 2 cups. Chill until slightly thickened. Fold in corn, onion, and pimiento and mix well. Pour into a wet 4-cup mold and chill until firm. Unmold and serve with lemon mayonnaise. Flavor with chutney, if desired. Makes 4 servings.

Fish Aspic

2 envelopes unflavored gelatin
2 cans (10½ ounces each) consommé or chicken broth
1 tablespoon lemon juice
½ teaspoon salt
¼ teaspoon freshly ground pepper
1 teaspoon dried dillweed
1 medium cucumber, peeled and diced
2 scallions, minced

1½ cups flaked cooked fish
   Shredded lettuce
   Lemon French Dressing* or Lemon Mayonnaise*

Soften the gelatin in ¼ cup cold consommé or broth. Add remaining broth; heat and stir to dissolve. Add lemon juice, salt, pepper, and dillweed. Chill until thick and syrupy. Fold in the cucumbers, scallions, and fish and pour into a wet 6-cup mold. Unmold on shredded lettuce and serve with lemon french dressing or lemon mayonnaise. Makes 6 to 8 servings.

Jellied Tuna-Buttermilk Salad

 1 envelope unflavored gelatin
 ¼ cup cold water
1¼ cups buttermilk
 ½ teaspoon dry mustard
 ½ teaspoon salt
 1 teaspoon grated onion
 1 tablespoon lemon juice
 ½ cup diced celery
 1 can (7 ounces) tuna, drained and flaked
   Salad greens
   Cucumber slices
   Green French Dressing*

Soften the gelatin in cold water, add ½ cup buttermilk; heat and stir until gelatin is dissolved. Add mustard, salt, onion, lemon juice, and remaining buttermilk. Chill until syrupy. Fold in the celery and tuna and pour into a wet 6-cup mold. Chill until firm. Unmold on greens and garnish with cucumber slices. Serve with dressing. Makes 4 to 6 servings.

Salmon Salad Mold

 1 can (1 pound) salmon
 2 envelopes unflavored gelatin
   Juice of 1 lemon
 1 tablespoon minced onion
 2 cups Mayonnaise*
 2 hard-cooked eggs, chopped
 2 tablespoons capers
 ⅓ cup chopped pimiento-stuffed olives
   Watercress
   Lemon French Dressing*

Drain salmon liquid into measuring cup. Add enough cold water to make ¼ cup liquid. Sprinkle with gelatin. When gelatin is softened, dissolve over very low heat. Add lemon juice and onion and cool. Stir into mayonnaise. Fold in flaked salmon, eggs, capers, and olives. Pour into a wet 6-cup mold and chill until firm. Unmold on a watercress-lined serving dish and serve with dressing. Makes 4 to 6 servings.

Ham Aspic

 1 envelope unflavored gelatin
 ¼ cup cold water
 1 cup hot tomato juice
 1 teaspoon prepared mustard
 1 teaspoon salt
 ½ teaspoon freshly ground pepper
 1 teaspoon lemon juice
 1 pound ham, minced
 ¼ cup minced onion
 ½ cup minced celery

Shredded lettuce
Louis Dressing*

Soften the gelatin in cold water and dissolve in hot tomato juice. Stir in mustard, salt, pepper, and lemon juice, and chill until syrupy. Add the ham, onion, and celery and mix thoroughly. Pour into a wet 1-quart mold and chill until firm. Unmold on a platter of shredded lettuce and serve with dressing. Makes 4 servings.

Jellied Turkey Salad

        2 envelopes unflavored gelatin
      ½ cup cold water
    2½ cups chicken broth
        1 tablespoon lemon juice
      ½ teaspoon salt
      ¼ teaspoon white pepper
        3 cups diced cooked turkey
      ½ cup minced celery
      ½ cup minced scallions
          Mayonnaise*
          Lemon wedges

Soften the gelatin in cold water. Add the broth and stir over low heat until the gelatin is dissolved. Add lemon juice, salt, and pepper. Chill until syrupy. Fold in the turkey, celery, and scallions. Pour into a wet loaf pan or 8-cup mold and chill until firm. Unmold on a cold plate and serve with mayonnaise and lemon wedges. Makes 8 servings.

Molded Veal-Cheese Salad

    2 envelopes unflavored gelatin
   ½ cup cold water
    1 cup chicken broth
    1 cup creamed cottage cheese
 1½ cups minced cooked veal
   ¼ cup chopped red or green pepper
   ½ cup chopped peeled cucumber
   ½ teaspoon salt
   ¼ teaspoon freshly ground pepper
     Chicory
     Mustard Mayonnaise*

Sprinkle gelatin over ½ cup cold water in saucepan. Add broth; cook and stir over low heat until gelatin dissolves. Cool slightly. Beat in cottage cheese and chill until syrupy. Fold in veal, chopped pepper, and cucumber, and season with salt and pepper. Pour into a wet loaf pan or a 6-cup mold. Chill until set. Unmold, garnish with chicory, and serve with mustard mayonnaise. Makes 6 servings.

Tomato Aspic

    1 envelope unflavored gelatin
   ½ cup cold water
    1 teaspoon sugar
 1½ cups vegetable juice cocktail
    1 teaspoon Worcestershire sauce
    1 teaspoon lemon juice
     Dash of hot pepper sauce
   ¼ cup chopped green onion
     Crisp greens
     French Dressing*

Sprinkle gelatin over cold water in small saucepan. Cook and stir over low heat until gelatin dissolves, about 3 minutes. Remove from heat and stir in sugar, juice cocktail, Worcestershire, lemon juice, and hot pepper sauce. Chill until thickened and very syrupy. Fold in onion. Turn into 4 individual ½-cup molds and chill until firm. Unmold on greens and serve with french dressing. Makes 4 servings.

Tomato-Chili-Cheese Jellied Salad

      2 tablespoons lemon juice
     ¼ cup cold water
      2 envelopes unflavored gelatin
      2 cups tomato juice
     ½ cup minced green pepper
      2 tablespoons grated onion
     ½ teaspoon chili powder
     ¼ teaspoon basil
     ¼ teaspoon salt
      2 tablespoons sugar
      1 can (15 ounces) chili with beans
      1 cup shredded Cheddar cheese
        Lettuce cups
        Green-pepper rings
        Mayonnaise*

Mix lemon juice and cold water and sprinkle with gelatin. Heat tomato juice just to boiling, add softened gelatin, and stir until dissolved. Add green pepper, onion, chili powder, basil, salt, and sugar. Chill in refrigerator or over ice until partially thickened. Fold in chili and cheese. Pour into a wet 8-inch square pan and chill until firm. Unmold, cut into squares, and serve in lettuce cups. Garnish with green-pepper rings and serve with mayonnaise. Makes 8 servings.

Molded Sweet-Sour Vegetable Salad

   2 envelopes unflavored gelatin
   1 cup cold water
  ½ cup sugar
   1 teaspoon salt
1½ cups ice water
  ½ cup vinegar
   2 tablespoons lemon juice
1½ cups finely shredded cabbage
   1 can (8 ounces) whole kernel corn, drained
   1 pimiento, finely chopped
   1 tablespoon finely chopped green pepper
      Crisp greens
      Preferred salad dressing

Sprinkle gelatin over cold water in small saucepan. Cook and stir over low heat until gelatin dissolves, about 3 minutes. Remove from heat and stir in sugar and salt until dissolved. Add ice water, vinegar, and lemon juice. Chill until thickened and very syrupy. Fold in cabbage, corn, pimiento, and green pepper. Turn into a wet 6-cup mold and chill until firm. Unmold on serving plate, garnish with greens, and serve with salad dressing. Makes 4 to 6 servings.

Vegetable-Yogurt Salad Mold

    2 envelopes unflavored gelatin
    ½ cup cold water
    1 tablespoon minced onion
    1 cup chicken bouillon
    ½ teaspoon salt
    ½ teaspoon dillweed
    8 ounces plain yogurt
    ½ cup sliced radishes
    ½ cup chopped green onion
    ½ cup shredded carrot
      Crisp greens

Sprinkle gelatin over cold water in small saucepan. Cook
and stir over low heat until gelatin dissolves, about 3
minutes. Remove from heat and add onion, bouillon, salt,
and dillweed. Stir in yogurt until thoroughly blended.
Add radishes, green onion, and carrot and mix well. Turn
into 6 wet 8-ounce molds and chill until firm. Unmold on
greens. Makes 6 servings.

ELEVEN

The Dessert Salad

A well-chosen dessert salad can be light—carrot-orange salad; or rich—peaches and blueberries in sour cream; sweet—mandarin oranges and bananas; or tangy—apple-cheese salad.

Fruit, the basis of dessert salads, can be served whole or sliced, with liqueur or cream, in aspics, with dessert dressings such as fruit mayonnaise, in molded salads, mousses, or frozen desserts. Cool salads of melon rings filled with fresh strawberries, mixed fresh fruit in crystal bowls, or pears and grapes in a jewellike mold are delightful, refreshing conclusions to any meal.

Apple-Cheese Salad

    2 large red apples, cored and diced
    1 cup thinly sliced celery
    ¾ cup drained pineapple tidbits
    ½ cup diced Cheddar cheese
    ¼ cup Mayonnaise*
    ¼ cup dairy sour cream
    1 teaspoon tarragon vinegar
    1 tablespoon prepared horseradish
      Salad greens

Mix apples, celery, pineapple, and cheese in a bowl. Blend mayonnaise, sour cream, vinegar, and horseradish. Combine with salad. Toss well and serve on greens. Makes 4 servings.

Molded Apple Salad

    2 envelopes unflavored gelatin
   ¼ cup cold water
1 ½ cups hot water
    2 tablespoons lemon juice
   ¼ teaspoon salt
    6 tablespoons brown sugar
    1 cup finely diced unpeeled red apple
   ½ cup snipped pitted dates
   ½ cup coarsely chopped walnuts
   ¼ cup diced celery
    2 tablespoons Mayonnaise*
   ½ cup heavy cream
     Salad greens

Soften gelatin in ¼ cup cold water, then dissolve in 1½ cups hot water. Stir in lemon juice, salt, and brown sugar and pour about ¼ cup into 1½-quart mold. Add about ¼ cup diced apple and chill until firm. Chill remaining gelatin until thickened but not firm. Mix remaining apple with dates, walnuts, celery, and mayonnaise. Whip cream and combine with apple mixture. Then fold into gelatin mixture. Pour into mold and chill until firm. Unmold on greens. Makes 4 to 6 servings.

Apricot-Banana Mold

  2 cups orange juice
  1 package (3 ounces) apricot or orange gelatin
  1 tablespoon lemon juice
  1 can (8¾ ounces) apricot halves, drained and
      cut up
 ½ banana, sliced
 ¼ cup chopped pecans
    Crisp greens
    Yogurt Fruit Salad Dressing*

Heat orange juice to boiling and pour over gelatin; stir until completely dissolved. Stir in lemon juice. Chill until thickened and syrupy. Fold in apricots, banana, and nuts. Turn into a wet 4-cup mold and chill until firm. Unmold on greens and serve with dressing. Makes 4 servings.

Carrot-Orange Salad

  3 tablespoons salad oil
  2 tablespoons cider vinegar or lemon juice
 ½ teaspoon salt
 ¼ teaspoon white pepper
  6 large carrots, coarsely shredded
  3 oranges, peeled, sectioned, and cut up
  2 tablespoons fresh snipped chives
  2 tablespoons orange liqueur
    Watercress sprigs

Mix oil, vinegar, salt, and pepper. Pour over carrots, oranges, and chives and toss lightly with the liqueur. Chill. Garnish with watercress. Makes 4 to 6 servings.

Citrus-Avocado Salad

Watercress sprigs
1 large avocado, peeled, pitted, and sliced
1 cup grapefruit sections, chilled
1 can (11 ounces) mandarin oranges, drained and chilled
½ cup Honey-Poppy Seed Dressing*

Arrange the watercress on 4 salad plates. Place slices of avocado down the center of each plate, and grapefruit and orange sections on either side of the avocado. Pour 2 tablespoons dressing over each salad. Makes 4 servings.

Cranberry Fruit Mold

2 envelopes unflavored gelatin
½ cup cold water
½ cup boiling orange juice
1 cup canned crushed pineapple, drained
1 tablespoon lemon juice
½ cup sugar
2 cups raw cranberries, ground
1 orange, peeled and diced
¼ cup coarsely chopped pecans or walnuts
Lettuce (optional)

Soften the gelatin in cold water and dissolve in boiling orange juice. Drain the pineapple and add the gelatin mixture, lemon juice, and sugar; stir until sugar dissolves. Chill until syrupy. Mix the cranberries with the pineapple, orange, and nuts. Fold the fruit mixture into the syrupy gelatin and pour into a wet 6-cup mold. Chill until firm. Unmold on a plate or lettuce-lined serving dish. Makes 4 servings.

Grape-Pineapple Molded Salad

    2 envelopes unflavored gelatin
    2 cups grape juice
    1 cup halved seedless grapes
    1 can (8 ounces) crushed pineapple, drained
    ½ cup dairy sour cream
      Mixed greens
      Roquefort Dressing*

In a small saucepan, soften gelatin in 1 cup cold grape juice. Place over low heat, stirring until gelatin dissolves, about 3 minutes. Pour into a mixing bowl, add remaining grape juice, and chill until slightly thickened. Fold in grapes, pineapple, and sour cream and pour into a wet 5-cup mold. Chill until firm. Unmold on a platter of mixed greens and serve with dressing. Makes 4 servings.

Kumquat, Chinese Cabbage, and Apple Salad

    8 preserved kumquats, cut up
    3 cups packed shredded Chinese cabbage
    2 medium red apples, unpeeled and cut in
        wedges
    2 tablespoons soy sauce
    2 tablespoons lemon juice
    ¼ teaspoon powdered or ½ teaspoon grated
        fresh ginger
    3 tablespoons vegetable oil
    3 tablespoons liquid from kumquats
    2 tablespoons minced parlsey

Drain the kumquats and reserve the liquid. Combine the kumquats, cabbage, and apples in a bowl. Mix together soy sauce, lemon juice, ginger, oil, and liquid from the kumquats. Add to the salad and toss. Serve in a glass bowl garnished with parsley. Makes 4 servings.

Mandarin-Orange and Banana Salad

¼ cup white raisins
1 can (11 ounces) mandarin oranges, chilled
  and drained
3 bananas, sliced
8 ounces lemon-flavored yogurt
Wheat germ or chopped walnuts

Place raisins in a cup with a few tablespoons hot water. Let stand 5 minutes to plump them; drain. Combine raisins with oranges and bananas. Gently toss with yogurt. Serve in individual bowls garnished with wheat germ or chopped nuts. Makes 4 servings.

Peaches and Blueberries in Sour Cream

5 large peaches, peeled and cut into ½-inch slices
1 pint blueberries, rinsed
½ cup packed brown sugar
1 cup dairy sour cream
Heavy cream (optional)

Place peaches and blueberries in a serving bowl. Combine brown sugar and sour cream. Mix into fruit; cover and chill. Serve with a pitcher of heavy cream and additional brown sugar, if desired. Makes 4 to 6 servings.

Pear and Cheddar-Cheese Salad

    12 chilled pear halves, fresh or canned
        Orange or lemon juice
     6 lettuce leaves
  1½ cups grated Cheddar cheese
  1½ cups Fruit French Dressing*

If using fresh pears, peel, halve them, and sprinkle with a little citrus juice to prevent discoloration. Place the pears on 6 individual plates on lettuce leaves. Fill the centers with cheese and pour 2 tablespoons dressing over each salad. Makes 6 servings.

Sparkling Pear-Grape Mold

     1 envelope unflavored gelatin
    ½ cup cold water
    ¼ cup sugar
    ½ teaspoon salt
     1 tablespoon lemon juice
     1 cup ginger ale
    ¾ cup (1 medium) diced fresh pear
    ¾ cup red grapes, halved and seeded
    ¼ cup chopped pecans
        Crisp greens
        Fruit Mayonnaise*

Sprinkle gelatin over cold water in small saucepan. Cook and stir over low heat until gelatin dissolves, about 3 minutes. Remove from heat and stir in sugar, salt, and lemon juice until sugar dissolves. Add ginger ale. Chill until thickened and very syrupy. Fold in pear, grapes, and nuts. Turn into a wet 3-cup mold and chill until firm.

Unmold on greens and serve with fruit mayonnaise. Makes 4 servings.

Peanut-Pear Salad

   1 package (8 ounces) cream cheese, softened
  ¼ cup smooth peanut butter
     Finely chopped peanuts
   8 peeled fresh or canned drained pear halves,
       chilled
     Salad greens
     Fruit Mayonnaise*

Mix cheese and peanut butter thoroughly. Shape into 8 balls, and roll in peanuts. Arrange 2 pear halves on each of 4 salad plates lined with greens. Place a cheese ball in the center of each pear half and serve with fruit mayonnaise. Makes 4 servings.

Molded Pineapple-Cheddar Cheese Salad

   2 envelopes unflavored gelatin
  ½ cup cold water
   1 can (1 pound) crushed pineapple
  ⅓ cup sugar
   1 tablespoon lemon juice
  ⅓ pound Cheddar cheese, grated
  ½ cup heavy cream, whipped

Soften the gelatin in cold water. Heat the pineapple with its juice. Add to gelatin and stir until gelatin is dissolved.

Immediately add sugar and lemon juice; stir well. Chill until syrupy. Fold in the cheese and whipped cream. Pour into a wet 6-cup mold and chill until firm. Makes 6 servings.

Prune-Cheese Tossed Salad

    3 cups torn assorted salad greens
    1 cup pitted prunes, cut up
    1 cup diced mozzarella cheese
    1 cup Yogurt Dressing*
    ¼ cup toasted slivered almonds

Combine the greens, prunes, and cheese in a salad bowl. Add the dressing and toss gently. Sprinkle with almonds. Makes 4 servings.

Watercress, Orange, and Shallot Salad

    2 bunches watercress
    3 large oranges, peeled and sliced or
        sectioned
    2 tablespoons chopped shallots
    1 teaspoon curry powder
    2 teaspoons sugar
    ½ cup Lemon French Dressing*

Remove the heavy stems of the cress and break up the large sprigs. Place in a serving bowl with the oranges and shallots. Add curry and sugar to the dressing and pour over the salad. Toss gently. Makes 6 servings.

Watermelon-Celery-Nut Salad

  2 packages (3 ounces each) cream cheese,
      softened
¼ cup Mayonnaise*
½ cup heavy cream, whipped
  2 cups diced celery
  3 cups watermelon balls or cubes
    Salad greens
½ cup chopped nuts

Beat cream cheese with mayonnaise until smooth and
fluffy. Fold into whipped cream and add celery. Arrange
watermelon on salad greens and top with cheese mixture.
Sprinkle with nuts. Makes 6 servings.

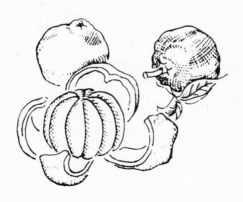

TWELVE

Party Desserts

What is a party without a colorful array of mouth-watering desserts? The following dessert salads will please the palate and delight the eye, lending a festive air to any special event—from a Fourth of July picnic buffet to a political fund-raising dinner.

Cottage Cheese-Fruit-Salad Platter

1 medium melon (cantaloupe, honeydew, or other)
1 pineapple
1 basket (12 ounces) strawberries
2 tablespoons confectioners' sugar
2 pears, cored, peeled, and sliced
3 bananas, peeled and sliced diagonally
Lemon or lime juice
3 cups shredded salad greens (Boston, Bibb, or other lettuce)
3 oranges, peeled and sliced crosswise
2 cups creamed cottage cheese
½ cup dairy sour cream
1 tablespoon grated orange rind
Honey-Lime Dressing* or Fruit Mayonnaise*

Peel, seed, and dice melon and set aside. Remove leaves and end piece from pineapple; peel and cut fruit into
198

1-inch rings; core, cut rings in half, and set aside. Hull strawberries, halve, and toss gently with confectioners' sugar. Sprinkle pears and bananas with lemon juice, cover tight with plastic wrap, and refrigerate. Arrange a bed of greens on a large platter with a halo of pineapple half-rings around the edge. Arrange remaining fruit in wedges in center of platter. Combine cottage cheese, sour cream, and orange rind and mound in center, if space is available, or serve in a bowl as an accompaniment. Serve with dressing. Makes 8 servings.

Summer Fruit Platter for a Party

1 large honeydew, casaba, or cantaloupe
    melon
1 pint blueberries, rinsed
1 pint strawberries, rinsed and hulled
1 pint raspberries
1 pound seedless green grapes, removed from
    stem
1 pound peaches, peeled and sliced
    Powdered sugar
1 quart of lime or lemon sherbet
2 cups Yogurt Fruit Salad Dressing,* dairy sour
    cream or whipped cream

Make balls from the melon flesh. Scoop out remaining melon and freeze the two halves. When ready to prepare the dessert, arrange mounds of blueberries, strawberries, raspberries, grapes, and peaches on a large serving platter. Sprinkle the fruit with a little powdered sugar. Fill one melon half with sherbet and the other with yogurt dressing or cream. Makes 12 servings.

Winter Fruit Platter with Grape-Lime Mold

1 package (6 ounces) lime gelatin
1 cup boiling water
1 cup ice water
1 cup cold ginger ale
1 tablespoon lemon juice
½ cup sugar
1 cup seedless or red or white seeded grapes, halved
1 cup dairy sour cream

Fruit:
16 prunes
3 pears, cored and sliced into wedges
2 red apples, unpeeled and cut into ½-inch wedges
3 bananas, cut into 1-inch pieces
Lemon juice
1 jar (1 pound) spiced peaches, sliced

Stir the gelatin into boiling water until dissolved. Add the ice water, ginger ale, 1 tablespoon lemon juice, and sugar, and stir. Pour about ¼ cup into a wet 6-cup mold and chill until almost set. Place a layer of the grapes on the gelatin and cover them with more gelatin. Refrigerate mold. Chill remaining gelatin until syrupy. Stir the sour cream into syrupy gelatin; pour into the mold and chill until firm. Soak the prunes in a little hot water to plump them. Brush the pears, apples, and bananas with lemon juice to prevent discoloration. Unmold the gelatin onto the center of a large serving platter. Arrange the pears, apples, bananas, prunes, and spiced peaches in separate piles around the molded salad. Makes 8 to 10 servings.

Frozen Apple-Citrus Salad

3 cups apple sauce
½ cup orange juice
¼ cup lemon juice
4 egg whites, beaten stiff
6 tablespoons sugar
Sliced fresh fruit

Combine the apple sauce with orange and lemon juice. Blend and put in freezer until frozen around the edges and mushy in the center. Remove from freezer and place in a bowl. Beat the egg whites until soft peaks form; beat in the sugar one tablespoon at a time. Fold this meringue into the apple mixture and refreeze in an 8-cup mold until firm. Serve garnished with fresh fruit. Makes 8 servings.

Frozen Fruit Salad

1 envelope unflavored gelatin
1⅓ cups syrup, drained from the canned fruits
Juice of 1 lemon
¼ teaspoon salt
¼ teaspoon ground ginger
½ cup drained crushed pineapple
1 cup drained canned sliced peaches
1 cup diced drained canned pears
1 cup sliced fresh or frozen strawberries
1 cup heavy cream, whipped
⅓ cup Mayonnaise*
Fresh mint leaves

Soften gelatin in ⅓ cup cold syrup and dissolve over low heat. Add remaining syrup, lemon juice, salt, ginger, pineapple, peaches, pears, and strawberries. Chill until slightly thickened. Mix cream and mayonnaise and fold into fruit mixture. Pour into two 1-quart trays or an 8-cup loaf pan and freeze until firm. Turn out of trays or pan and cut into slices. Garnish with fresh mint. Makes 8 to 10 servings.

Frozen Pineapple-Date Salad

      1 pint small-curd cottage cheese
     ½ cup honey
    2½ cups crushed pineapple, drained, reserve
          liquid
      1 cup coarsely chopped dates
      1 cup heavy cream, whipped, or 1 cup
          Mayonnaise*

Smooth the cheese and blend in the honey and liquid from the pineapple. Add the pineapple and dates and mix thoroughly. Fold in the cream or mayonnaise and freeze in an 8-cup mold until firm. Makes 8 to 10 servings.

Cherry-Orange Charlotte

      2 envelopes unflavored gelatin
      1 cup sugar
      1 cup cold water
    1½ cups orange juice
      6 tablespoons lemon juice
      4 egg whites
      1 cup heavy cream, whipped
          Cherry Sauce
          Green Leaves
          Fresh dark sweet cherries

In small saucepan, mix gelatin and sugar. Add 1 cup cold water and put over low heat, stirring until gelatin is dissolved. Cool slightly, then add orange and lemon juices. Chill until mixture begins to set. Beat egg whites until soft peaks form. Fold into gelatin mixture; then fold in whipped cream. Turn into a wet 2-quart mold and chill until set. Unmold on a serving plate and pour cherry sauce over the top. Decorate with leaves and cherries. Makes 8 to 10 servings.

Cherry Sauce: Halve and pit about 3 cups fresh dark sweet cherries (this can be done earlier). Shortly before serving, mix with light corn syrup and sugar to taste.

Green Leaves: Mix almond paste with enough sugar to create right consistency to roll. Add a little green food coloring. Roll out on waxed paper, cut in shape of leaves with pastry wheel, and make veins with knife. Put over handle of wooden spoon to shape and dry. Store in airtight container.

Spiced Peach Salad Mold

10 spiced peach halves, reserve liquid
1 package (6 ounces) peach gelatin
2 cups boiling water
  Reserved liquid and water
4 tablespoons brown sugar
4 tablespoons rum or brandy
2 cups dairy sour cream

Drain the peaches and cut them into bite-size pieces. Dissolve the gelatin in boiling water. Add liquid from the peaches and enough water to make 2 cups. Stir in peaches and pour into a wet 2-quart mold. Chill until firm. Blend the brown sugar and rum or brandy into the sour cream. Refrigerate. Unmold the salad and spoon the sour cream mixture over the peach mold. Makes 8 servings.

Pineapple and Strawberries in the Half Shell

    1 large pineapple
    2 pints strawberries
      Powdered sugar
   12 to 16 large black cherries
      Fruit Mayonnaise* or Yogurt Nut Dressing*

Cut the pineapple in half lengthwise through the leaves. Scoop out the flesh and cut it into bite-size pieces. Scallop the edges of the pineapple shells, if desired, and freeze them. Rinse and hull the strawberries, add sugar to taste, and combine them with the pineapple; chill. When ready to serve the fruit, spread the pineapple leaves slightly apart and force the cherries here and there in between. Fill the shells with the chilled fruit and serve with dressing. Makes 6 to 8 servings.

Tropical Fruit Salad Bowl

1 jar (8 ounces) kumquats, reserve liquid
1 pineapple, peeled and cut into bite-size
    pieces
3 bananas, sliced
3 kiwi fruit, peeled and sliced into rounds
1 large papaya, cut up
1 mango, cut up
2 cups melon balls
2 tablespoons lemon juice
6 tablespoons rum, preferably dark
    Shredded coconut

Drain the kumquats. Combine the kumquats, pineapple, bananas, kiwi fruit, papaya, mango, and melon balls in a glass serving bowl. Mix the kumquat juice with the lemon juice and rum. Pour over the fruit, toss gently, and chill for an hour or more. Garnish with coconut. Makes 12 servings.

Salad Dressing

An excellent salad should wear a dressing that not only binds the fruit or vegetables together and adds food value, but best enhances the flavor of its ingredients.

Ignore the variety of dressings on supermarket shelves and do make your own. They taste better, are less expensive, and take very little time. Make dressings several hours in advance so the flavors have time to blend. Shake or whip them again before serving. A dressing should coat a salad. If there's a pool at the bottom of your salad bowl, you'll find you have too much of a good thing.

There are three basic types of dressings: french, called vinaigrette in France, mayonnaise, and cooked or boiled dressing.

French dressing, the easiest and most popular, consists of oil, vinegar, salt, pepper, and often mustard and sometimes garlic. With garlic it is usually called Italian. There are many varieties of this dressing, although none bear any resemblance to the thick, sweet, pink mixture sold commerically as "French Dressing." If you like a strong flavor, use all or part olive oil. For a subtler version part corn, soy, vegetable, or peanut oils are excellent. Safflower oil is not only cholesterol-free, but it acts to break up cholesterol in the body. Experiment with vinegar—red or white wine, cider, herb, or malt. Make your own herb varieties by adding a sprig of fresh tarragon, basil, dill, or a garlic clove to your favorite vinegar.

Don't be afraid to make your own mayonnaise. Relax and follow the recipes carefully. For a lighter texture use a blender or food processor. It takes a little longer to make mayonnaise by hand, but the results are a richer dressing and well worth the effort.

Cooked dressing is less rich than mayonnaise, which it resembles in texture. It is made with milk rather than oil and is popular with calorie-counters. It can be substituted for mayonnaise in some recipes and is especially good on slaws and fish salads. Cottage cheese and yogurt dressings are light, also oil-free, and low in calories.

Still there may be occasions when you will need to use a commercial salad dressing. Avoid highly seasoned ones so that you can flavor them yourself. Included is a chart entitled "Tips for Personalizing Commercial Dressings" to help you enliven the bland varieties to suit yourself and your salad.

French Dressing (French Vinaigrette)

¼ cup wine vinegar
½ teaspoon salt
¼ teaspoon freshly ground pepper
¾ cup olive oil

Put the vinegar and salt and pepper in a bowl or jar. Add the oil slowly and mix thoroughly. If using a jar, cover and shake. Mix again just before serving. Makes 1 cup.

VARIATIONS

ANCHOVY FRENCH DRESSING: Add 2 fillets of anchovies, minced, and ½ clove crushed garlic to French Dressing.*

HERB FRENCH DRESSING: Add ½ teaspoon tarragon, ½ teaspoon basil or oregano, and 1 teaspoon minced parsley to French Dressing.*

MUSTARD FRENCH DRESSING: Add ½ teaspoon dry or 1 teaspoon prepared mustard to French Dressing.*

GARLIC FRENCH DRESSING: Add 1 small to medium clove crushed garlic to Mustard French Dressing.*

GREEN FRENCH DRESSING: Add ½ cup minced parsley to French Dressing* and whirl in a blender.

PIMIENTO FRENCH DRESSING: Add one drained, minced pimiento to French Dressing.*

Lemon French Dressing

½ teaspoon salt
1 teaspoon sugar, for vegetable salads, or 1
      tablespoon sugar, for dessert salads
3 tablespoons lemon juice
½ cup oil, part or all olive

Stir the salt and sugar with the lemon juice. Pour in the oil slowly while stirring vigorously. Makes ¾ cup.

Vinaigrette (*American Vinaigrette*)

¼ cup wine vinegar
¾ cup oil, part olive
1 teaspoon salt
¼ teaspoon freshly ground pepper
¼ teaspoon paprika
½ teaspoon sugar
1 tablespoon minced chives

1 tablespoon minced parsley
1 tablespoon chopped dill pickle
1 hard-cooked egg, grated

Combine the vinegar, oil, salt, pepper, paprika, and sugar. Mix thoroughly. Add the chives, parsley, and pickle and stir well. Fold in the grated egg. Chill. Makes 1¼ cups.

Avocado Dressing

½ cup olive or salad oil
¼ cup lemon juice
1 small clove garlic, crushed
¼ teaspoon salt
1 small avocado, diced

Combine the oil, lemon juice, garlic, salt, and avocado in a blender and whirl until smooth. Serve at once or sprinkle with lemon juice, cover tight with plastic wrap, and refrigerate. Makes 1¼ cups.

Blue Cheese and Wine Dressing

¼ cup white wine
1 tablespoon lemon juice
3 tablespoons oil, part olive
¼ pound blue cheese, crumbled
Salt
Freshly ground pepper

Mix wine, lemon juice, and oil thoroughly. Add the cheese and stir gently. Season to taste with salt and pepper. Makes ¾ cup.

Herbed Italian Dressing

    3 tablespoons wine vinegar
    ¾ cup olive oil
    1 clove garlic, minced or crushed
    1 tablespoon minced onion
    2 teaspoons chopped fresh basil or ½
        teaspoon dried
    ½ teaspoon dried oregano
    ½ teaspoon salt
    ¼ teaspoon freshly ground pepper

Place the vinegar in a bowl and stir in the oil slowly while beating. When all of the oil is absorbed, add the garlic, onion, herbs, salt, and pepper. Mix thoroughly. Makes 1 cup.

Lorenzo Dressing

    ¾ cup olive oil
    ¼ cup vinegar
    ½ teaspoon salt
    ¼ teaspoon freshly ground pepper
    ⅓ cup chili sauce
    1 cup finely chopped watercress leaves

Combine the oil, vinegar, salt, pepper, and chili sauce and mix well. Stir in the watercress. This dressing should be quite thick. Makes 2⅓ cups.

Spicy Dressing

½ teaspoon salt
½ teaspoon freshly ground pepper
½ teaspoon paprika
½ teaspoon sugar
½ teaspoon dry mustard
1 tablespoon celery seed
½ teaspoon curry
½ teaspoon tarragon
¼ cup wine vinegar
1 teaspoon Worcestershire sauce
Dash hot pepper sauce
½ cup salad oil

Combine salt, pepper, paprika, sugar, mustard, celery seed, curry, and tarragon. Mix vinegar, Worcestershire sauce, and hot pepper sauce and stir into the dry ingredients. Add the oil slowly, stirring steadily, until it is totally absorbed. Makes ¾ cup.

Cooked Salad Dressing

1 teaspoon salt
½ teaspoon white pepper
2 tablespoons flour
1 tablespoon sugar
1 teaspoon dry mustard
1 cup milk
2 eggs, beaten
¼ cup vinegar
1 tablespoon butter

Combine the salt, pepper, flour, sugar, and mustard in a double boiler. Using a whisk blend the milk with dry ingredients until smooth. Cook over medium heat and stir until thickened. Add the beaten eggs one at a time while continuing to cook and stir. Stir in the vinegar very slowly. Beat in butter. Remove from heat and cool. Cover with plastic wrap and chill. Makes 1½ cups.

Indonesian Peanut Sauce

¼ cup minced onion
1 tablespoon butter
1 cup water
½ cup peanut butter
1 tablespoon lemon juice
½ teaspoon salt
¼ to ½ teaspoon crushed dried red peppers

Sauté the onion in butter until tender but not brown. Combine the water and peanut butter and add to the onion. Stir until smooth. Season with lemon juice, salt, and the crushed red peppers. Chill. Makes 1¾ cups.

Mayonnaise

1 egg yolk
½ teaspoon salt
¼ teaspoon dry mustard
1 cup oil, at least ½ olive
2 tablespoons vinegar or lemon juice

Beat the egg yolk, salt, and mustard in a bowl. Add the oil, drop by drop, beating steadily with a whisk until the mixture thickens. Continue to stir while adding the remaining oil slowly in a very thin stream. When all the oil is absorbed, add vinegar or lemon juice and beat well. The mixture should be creamy and light-colored. Cover and refrigerate. Makes 1¼ cups.

NOTE: If the mayonnaise divides, stop. Place a yolk in another bowl and again add oil drop by drop. When mixture begins to thicken add the divided mayonnaise slowly while beating.

VARIATIONS

HERB MAYONNAISE: Add 2 teaspoons each minced chives and fresh parsley, 1 teaspoon each tarragon and dried basil to 1 cup Mayonnaise.*

HORSERADISH MAYONNAISE: Add ½ cup sour cream and 3 tablespoons prepared horseradish to 1 cup Mayonnaise.*

LEMON MAYONNAISE: Use lemon juice instead of vinegar in Mayonnaise.* Stir in an additional tablespoon of lemon juice and mix well.

MUSTARD MAYONNAISE: Add 1 tablespoon prepared mustard to 1 cup Mayonnaise* and mix thoroughly.

Blender Mayonnaise

    1 egg
    ½ teaspoon salt
    ¼ teaspoon dry mustard
    1 cup oil, ⅓ olive
    2 tablespoons vinegar or lemon juice

Put the whole egg, salt, mustard, and two tablespoons oil into a blender. Turn on the blender and add the remaining oil in a very slow stream. As mixture begins to thicken increase the stream. Add vinegar or lemon juice. Spoon into a bowl, taste for seasoning, and chill. Makes 1¼ cups.

PROCESSOR MAYONNAISE—Proceed as for Blender Mayonnaise and starting with ¼ cup of oil and running the machine only a few seconds at a time.

Frozen Tomato Mayonnaise

1 cup Mayonnaise*
1 cup minced tomato flesh, drained and seeded
½ teaspoon salt
¼ teaspoon red pepper
½ teaspoon sugar

Combine mayonnaise and tomato flesh. Add salt, pepper, and sugar and stir well. The mixture should be the consistency of custard. Freeze. Makes 2 cups.

Green Goddess Dressing

1 cup Mayonnaise*
2 tablespoons lemon juice
2 tablespoons tarragon vinegar
1 small clove garlic, crushed
4 anchovy fillets, minced
1 tablespoon minced scallion, green stem only
2 tablespoons minced chives
¼ cup finely minced parsley leaves
¼ teaspoon dried tarragon
Salt
Freshly ground pepper

Combine mayonnaise, lemon juice, vinegar, anchovies, scallions, chives, parsley, and tarragon in a mixing bowl or whirl in a blender until thoroughly mixed. Season to taste with salt and pepper. Makes 1⅓ cups.

Louis Dressing

   1 cup Lemon Mayonnaise*
  ¼ cup chili sauce
  2 tablespoons minced green pepper
  3 scallions, finely chopped
  ¼ cup heavy cream
    Dash hot pepper sauce
    Salt
    Freshly ground pepper

Place the mayonnaise in a bowl and combine with chili sauce, green pepper, scallions, cream, and hot pepper sauce. Blend well. Season with salt and pepper. Makes 1⅔ cups.

Creamy Roquefort Dressing

  ½ cup Mayonnaise*
  ½ cup dairy sour cream
  ¼ pound crumbled Roquefort cheese
  ½ teaspoon salt
  ¼ teaspoon freshly ground pepper
    Heavy cream

Combine the mayonnaise and sour cream; blend in the cheese, salt, and pepper. Thin with a little heavy cream if desired. Makes 1¼ cups.

Russian Dressing

   1 cup Mayonnaise*
  ⅓ cup chili sauce
   2 tablespoons lemon juice
   2 tablespoons minced pickles
   2 tablespoons minced scallions
   2 tablespoons black or red caviar

Combine mayonnaise, chili sauce, lemon juice, pickles, scallions, and caviar in a bowl and beat until thoroughly blended. Chill. Makes 1¾ cups.

Thousand Island Dressing

  ½ cup Mayonnaise*
  1 teaspoon prepared mustard
  ¼ cup chili sauce
  1 tablespoon minced parsley
  1 teaspoon Worcestershire sauce
  1 hard-cooked egg, chopped
    Salt
    Freshly ground pepper

Combine the mayonnaise, mustard, chili sauce, parsley, Worcestershire sauce, and egg. Mix thoroughly. Season with salt and pepper to taste. Makes 1 cup.

Cottage Cheese Dressing

  ½ cup creamed cottage cheese
  ¼ cup plain yogurt

    2 tablespoons wine vinegar
    1 teaspoon Worcestershire sauce
    2 tablespoons minced scallions
    2 tablespoons minced parsley
    ½ teaspoon salt
    ¼ teaspoon freshly ground pepper

Using a whisk, blender, or food processor, blend the cheese and yogurt together. Add vinegar, Worcestershire sauce, scallions, parsley, salt and pepper, and mix thoroughly. Makes 1 cup.

Horseradish Dressing

    ½ cup dairy sour cream
    2 tablespoons prepared horseradish
    ½ teaspoon sugar

Combine the sour cream with the horseradish and sugar and blend thoroughly. Makes ½ cup.

Yogurt Dressing

    1 cup plain yogurt
    1 clove garlic, crushed
    2 teaspoons lemon juice
    1 tablespoon minced onion
    ½ teaspoon salt

Combine yogurt, garlic, lemon juice, onion, and salt. Mix thoroughly in a bowl or in a blender. Makes 1 cup.

Yogurt-Peanut Dressing

2 tablespoons peanut butter
2 tablespoons salad oil
1 tablespoon lemon juice
1 teaspoon soy sauce
½ cup plain yogurt
1 tablespoon wheat germ

Put the peanut butter, oil, lemon juice, soy sauce, and yogurt in a blender or food processor and blend until smooth. Spoon into a bowl and add the wheat germ. Makes ¾ cup.

Honey-Lime Dressing

⅓ cup salad oil
⅓ cup lime juice
⅓ cup honey
Pinch of salt
1 tablespoon grated orange rind

Combine oil, lime juice, honey, salt, and orange rind in a blender or food processor and whirl until smooth. Makes 1 cup.

VARIATION

HONEY–POPPY-SEED DRESSING: Omit orange rind and add 1 tablespoon poppy-seed to Honey-Lime Dressing.*

Honey-Lemon Dressing

½ cup honey
½ teaspoon salt
1 teaspoon prepared mustard
1 teaspoon paprika
½ cup lemon juice
¾ cup salad oil

Mix honey, salt, mustard, paprika, lemon juice, and oil in a blender or beat with a rotary beater. Makes 1¾ cups.

Fruit French Dressing

1 tablespoon sugar
½ teaspoon salt
½ teaspoon curry powder (optional)
2 tablespoons lemon juice
1 tablespoon grapefruit juice
1 tablespoon orange juice
½ cup olive oil

Mix the sugar, salt, and the curry, if you wish. Add the fruit juices and stir thoroughly. Pour in the oil slowly while stirring. Makes ¾ cup.

Fruit Mayonnaise

½ cup Mayonnaise*
¼ cup dairy sour cream
2 tablespoons sherry
2 teaspoons lemon juice
1 tablespoon grapefruit juice
3 tablespoons pineapple juice
1 tablespoon sugar

Combine mayonnaise with sour cream. Add sherry, lemon juice, grapefruit juice, pineapple juice, and sugar and beat vigorously. Makes 1¼ cups.

Honey Lemon Mayonnaise

1 cup Mayonnaise*
⅓ cup honey
2 tablespoons lemon juice
¼ cup heavy cream

Combine mayonnaise, honey, lemon juice, and cream. Mix well. For a lighter dressing, whip the cream and fold it into the other ingredients. Makes 1¾ cups.

VARIATION

HONEY LIME MAYONNAISE: Substitute lime juice for the lemon juice in Honey Lemon Mayonnaise.*

Sherry Dessert Dressing

½ teaspoon salt
2 teaspoons sugar
1 tablespoon lemon juice
3 tablespoons sherry
½ cup oil

Place the salt, sugar, lemon juice, and sherry in a bowl and stir until sugar is dissolved. Add the oil gradually while stirring. Makes ¾ cup.

Yogurt Fruit Salad Dressing

3 tablespoons orange juice
1 tablespoon lemon juice
3 tablespoons peanut oil
½ cup plain yogurt
2 tablespoons honey
½ teaspoon cinnamon (optional)

Combine the orange and lemon juices with the oil and blend well. Mix the yogurt and honey and stir it into the dressing. Add the cinnamon, if you wish. Makes 1 cup.

Yogurt-Nut Dressing for Fruits

1 cup plain yogurt
2 tablespoons honey
2 tablespoons pineapple juice
3 tablespoons chopped walnuts

Mix the yogurt, honey, and pineapple juice thoroughly. Stir in the nuts. Makes 1¼ cups.

Tips for Personalizing Commercial Dressings

To 8 ounces of the following dressing, add and shake well before serving:

BLUE CHEESE   1 clove garlic, crushed
2 teaspoons Worcestershire sauce

CREAMY   1 teaspoon soy sauce
1 teaspoon Worcestershire sauce
1 tablespoon minced chives or scallions

FRENCH DRESSING   2 teaspoons lemon juice
(the thick kind)   2 teaspoons minced pickles
1 teaspoon pickle juice
1 teaspoon prepared mustard

ITALIAN   3 tablespoons grated Parmesan cheese

MAYONNAISE   2 teaspoons lemon juice, 1 teaspoon prepared mustard,
1 teaspoon dill

1 package (4 ounces) blue cheese mixed with 2 tablespoons sour cream and 1 teaspoon Worcestershire sauce

2 tablespoons orange juice, 1 tablespoon lemon juice,
1 tablespoon sugar (for fruits)

2 teaspoons blended salad herbs or 1 teaspoon each
chervil, parsley, dill, and chives

1 teaspoon lemon juice, 1 teaspoon curry, 1 clove
garlic, crushed

OIL AND VINEGAR   1 teaspoon curry, 2 teaspoons lemon juice

½ teaspoon sugar, 1 teaspoon tarragon or oregano, 2 teaspoons minced parsley

4 chopped anchovies, 2 teaspoons lemon juice, 1 teaspoon minced parsley

2 tablespoons chopped egg, 1 clove garlic, crushed, 1 tablespoon chili sauce

RUSSIAN   ¼ cup sour cream, a few drops hot pepper sauce, 1 tablespoon tomato sauce

THOUSAND ISLAND   1 teaspoon grated onion, ¼ teaspoon paprika, 1 tablespoon minced parsley

Index

225